OUR WONDERFUL WORLD.

AND WHAT WE CAN LEARN FROM IT

Also by Malcolm Edmunds:

Defence in Animals:
a Survey of Anti-predator Defences, 1974

North Atlantic Nudibranchs (Mollusca) seen by Henning
Lemche (with Hanne Just), 1985

Wildlife of Lancashire (edited with Tim Mitcham &
Geoff Morries), 2004

OUR WONDERFUL WORLD:

AND WHAT WE CAN LEARN FROM IT

Malcolm Edmunds

A CIP catalogue record for this book is available from the British Library.

ISBN 978-0-9954649-0-2

Book layout and cover design by Clare Brayshaw

Cover pictures

Front cover above: two of the Mediterranean bee-orchids, Ophrys dodekanensis (left) and Ophrys regis-ferdinandii, the eastern mirror orchid (right) (see Chapter 1 Flowers).

Front cover below: chimpanzees © Kristof Degreef | Dreamstime.com, Pan troglodytes (see Chapter 3 Primates).

Back cover: Another Mediterranean bee-orchid, Ophrys ferrum-equinum (see Chapter 1 Flowers).

Prepared and printed by:

York Publishing Services Ltd
64 Hallfield Road
Layerthorpe
York YO31 7ZQ

Tel: 01904 431213

Website: www.yps-publishing.co.uk

Table of Contents

OUR WONDERFUL WORLD:
AND WHAT WE CAN LEARN FROM IT

Preface

Over the past 30 years I have written a series of short essays on the natural world and lessons that we humans can learn from it. Many have been published in the weekly Quaker journal *The Friend* but some are original. Three of them were written by my wife Janet who also made valuable criticisms of all of my essays. A few are slightly longer than the published version. My aim has been to draw attention to lessons for human action and behaviour that we can learn from the natural world. As a professional zoologist I have drawn on my understanding of animal behaviour, ecology and evolution for many of the essays.

Chapter 1 looks at flowering plants which give us humans so much pleasure but which have evolved solely to attract pollinators, so this pleasure is purely incidental.

The next three Chapters look at animal behaviour and draw parallels with human behaviour. In many animals these behaviours have evolved independently, but in the case of the great apes, we may have inherited them from our pre-human ancestors.

Chapter 5 looks at Charles Darwin's theory of Evolution and also at our current understanding of

Evolution. It then cautions against some of the dangers as well as benefits of genetic engineering.

Chapter 6 looks at just a few places of fascination, interest and inspiration.

Chapter 7 is more serious and addresses the rapid growth of human population and its unsustainable use of limited world resources – an issue that will become more critical every year as the human population and its impact on the environment continue to rise.

CHAPTER 1

Flowers

The Beauty of Flowers

There is beauty in the colours, the shapes and the fragrance of flowers that uplifts my spirit and gives me great pleasure, be they in a well kept garden or growing wild in wood or meadow. Yet they were not created for our delight and our enjoyment. That myth is part of the nineteenth-century view that places us humans at the centre of creation, with all other animals and plants made for our delight, for our benefit, to do with them what we wish even if that means their destruction. No, wild flowers have just as much right to exist on Earth as we do, and we ignore this at our peril.

So why do flowers have such beauty? Unlike the peacock which can be seen by other peacocks and pea-hens, flowers cannot see one another, nor so far as we know, can they take pleasure in their beauty. They have evolved bright colours quite simply because these particular plants attracted more pollinators than did less gaudy flowers, and so they set more seed. Some, like the massed heads of cow parsley or daises, attract a variety of bees, flies, beetles and other insects which take nectar and in so doing transfer pollen from one flower to another. Others lure just one or a few pollinators and so avoid wastage of pollen being deposited on the wrong kind of plant: foxglove and monkshood are designed for pollination by bumblebees, while honeysuckle has nectar in a long spur which can only be reached by long-tongued moths. Almost all European flowers are blue, yellow, white or ultra-violet because these are the colours that insects can see, and very few are red. Many North American and tropical flowers are red and these are pollinated by birds such as the sunbirds of the Old World and the hummingbirds of the New. Flowers have bright colours, curious shapes and fragrant perfumes to attract pollinators. The fact that we enjoy them and wonder at their beauty is, for the flowers, quite incidental. Yet how wonderful it is that we can experience so much joy and pleasure from them.

Bumblebee orchid
(*Ophrys bombyliflora*)

But there is one lesson we can learn from flowers and their pollinators: that is the need for co-operation. Without this intimate relationship with an animal for mutual benefit, they would quickly die out along with the dodo and the dinosaurs. Are we aware that we too have to co-operate with each other, with other animals and plants, and even with the inanimate world? Of course there are cheats. There are some flowers that attract insects with colour and scent but then do not waste their own scarce resources by giving any nectar: the insect gets nothing but is 'used' by the plant to take pollen away to another flower. The remarkable bee and spider orchids attract males of particular species of wasp which mistake them for a mate, try to pair with the flower, and in so doing pick up pollen which they take to the next orchid flower they visit. And there are some short-tongued bees and birds that bore holes into the bases of long-spurred flowers to steal nectar without picking up any pollen. There are cheats too in our own society, people who try to exploit rather than co-operate, for their own personal benefit rather than for mutual benefit.

Lady's Slipper orchids
(*Cypripedium calceolus*)

Flowers have survived for millions of years because they co-operate. If we are to survive the next few centuries we too must co-operate and not simply exploit. The loss of even one species of flower is a loss of a part of the world, and scores of species are being lost every week as the tropical forests are destroyed in the name of progress and development.

Are we doing enough to help others to appreciate the beauty and diversity of nature and to promote the view that wild flowers have as much right to exist on this overcrowded world as we have? "Any man's death diminishes me, because I am involved in mankind; and therefore never send to know for whom the bell tolls, it tolls for thee". John Donne was surely right; yet it is not just the death of any man or woman that is important, but rather the wanton destruction of any form of life.

~

To give pleasure

In 1888, at the age of 17, my great uncle Fred followed his brother Albert out to Oregon. There he led an adventurous life, somewhat removed from his Quaker upbringing, joining the gold rush to Klondike and taking part in the war with the Philippines. He eventually settled down near Portland, Oregon, to become one of the leading rose growers of the north-west, then married and started a family when he was 52 years old. His business passed to his son, another Fred, and then to grandson Phil Edmunds. Yet I still remember from 40 years ago a fine red rose with a touch of yellow on the petals called after my great uncle 'Fred Edmunds'.

The beauty of a wild flower, whether it is the colour of a poppy, the form and delicacy of columbine, or the perfume and nectar filled tube of honeysuckle, owes nothing to the ingenuity of people: such beauty has evolved because it attracts some insect to pollinate it. So too with the wild rose of our hedgerows.

But the enormous double roses of our gardens are quite different. They, like sweet peas, dahlias and chrysanthemums, are the product of many years of careful selection and breeding by devoted men and women. Of course rose breeders can make a lot of money, but I very much doubt if making money is the reason why they take up this occupation. The colour, shape and form of the petals as well as the scent have been developed in order to give pleasure to other people.

This surely is something that we can all try to emulate: that one of the principal aims of our lives should be to try to give pleasure to people whom we may never meet. So, although I never met either him or his son, I can still give thanks for the life of great uncle Fred and of others like him who had a passion for breeding roses to give pleasure to people like me.

~

Monkshood

As I took the small vase of flowers to Quaker Meeting last summer I noticed that three of the six spikes of monkshood flowers were *upside down*. Monkshood has deep blue flowers and is closely related to the equally poisonous delphinium, but it has a large petal on the upper side of the flower shaped

Monkshood
(*Aconitum napellus*)

like the cowl of a monk – hence the common name. The flower is beautifully adapted to being pollinated by bumblebees which land on the base of the flower between the four lower petals (ok, botanists, I know these are technically sepals), surrounded by the stamens which dust them with pollen. The insect then reaches upwards with its long tongue to the nectaries high up under the hood. If it then visits a more mature flower in which the stamens have withered it will inadvertently deposit some of the pollen on the stigmas. Other solitary bees and honey-bees do not have a long enough tongue to reach the nectaries so they rarely visit the flowers. The hood-shaped upper petal also protects the sexual organs from the rain; but why did three of the six spikes have upside-down flowers?

Well, three of the flower spikes which I cut had thick stems and the flowers were normal with the hood uppermost, but the other three had thin stems and the weight of the large flowers caused them to hang down so that the flowers would be expected to have the hood at the bottom where any rain would fill it with water. However, although the stem was hanging down the flowers were all right way up. What had happened is that the flower buds were sufficiently heavy to cause the stem to bend down but then the flower stalks grew differentially on the upper and lower sides so that they rotated to bring the hood back to the top as the flowers opened fully and the flowers' sexual organs were protected from rain. What a remarkable adaptation – and all done with no trace of a nervous system let alone a brain and conscious thought.

We humans are not so very different from monkshood in that most of our everyday actions are automatic, either because they are innate or because we have learned them so that little or no conscious thought is required to carry them out. Yet we have the most highly developed brain of any animal. While we are becoming increasingly aware of the damage we are doing to our environment are we actually doing enough to minimise the harm that we inadvertently do? We need to engage our wonderful brain much more than most of us do to be aware of the suffering and needs of people around us and of the environment which we are all too rapidly destroying beyond repair.

~

Love-in-the-mist

A few Sundays back the Friend who brought flowers to Quaker Meeting included in her small posy three flower-heads of Love-in-the-mist (*Nigella damascena*). Love-in-the-mist has pale blue petals and delicate leaves and bracts, but these three flowers had shed all of their petals and the green seed capsules had each swollen to the diameter of a fifty pence coin with several branched horn-like projections. Because of this change of appearance, instead of being Love-in-the-mist, the seed head is sometimes called Devil-in-the-bush.

Quakers believe there is that of God in everyone, which means that all of us can be kind and loving, show generosity and compassion: we all of us have Love-in-the-mist. Three-hundred and fifty years ago the Quaker George Fox advised us to "Be patterns, be examples in all countries, places, islands, nations, wherever you come, that your carriage and life may preach among all sorts of people, and to them; then you will come to walk cheerfully over the world, answering that of God in everyone". But all too often instead of encountering Love-in-the-mist in ourselves and in others we encounter Devil-in-the-bush: feelings of resentment, dislike or even hatred, and wishing to get our own back. The challenge is to be aware of the Devil-in-the-bush in ourselves and in others, but to concentrate on encouraging the Love-in-the-mist even when it is hard to discern.

~

Double Flowers

A few months ago the flowers brought to Quaker Meeting were the lovely yellow *Kerria japonica*, also known as Jew's mantle or simply Kerria. As with most plants of this species the flowers were double almost spherical pompoms. Many of our favourite garden flowers are double, for example roses, carnations, dahlias and chrysanthemums. Horticulturalists and Garden Centres love to offer double flowers of a great many species to customers, often called 'floraplena' or 'pleniflora'. However double flowers often (though not always) have no stamens, or if these are present they are so buried amongst the petals that they are not accessible to insects. So while they are lovely in the garden or the flower vase they are useless for honey-bees, bumble-bees, scores of solitary bees, flies and other insects that visit in order to collect protein-rich pollen. If they lack nectar as well they are of no use for butterflies and moths either. So if you want to help our declining pollinating insects, in your garden, avoid too many double flowers. Double flowers are not 'normal', they are freaks and most could not survive and reproduce in the wild.

A few years back I looked round at the Friends in Meeting one Sunday and thought of them lovingly and of the ailments many of them had ranging from infirmity in old age to some temporary or chronic illness. If these Friends were plants they would be considered to be not 'normal'. Yet more than half of the Friends present suffered from some ailment or disability, so it would have been misleading to consider them abnormal; because of their numbers it was those with some disability who were the 'normal' members of the Meeting and the apparently 100% healthy few who were abnormal.

CHAPTER 2

Insects

Ants

Some fifty years ago our house at Achimota, in Ghana, had holes in the mosquito netting on the loo window through which several red weaver ants (*Oecophylla longinoda*) often came in. At night they would be on the look out for worker termites which were steadily eating away the window frame from the inside and which are an easy prey for the huge jaws of these vicious ants. On nocturnal visits to the loo we could hear the faint chewing of termite jaws in the window frame. Then one night instead of just a few ants the whole floor was a writhing mass of hundreds of fighting red ants. The loo was evidently on the boundary between two colonies of weaver ants and for some reason one colony was trying to extend its boundary with the result that there was a massive battle. By morning the room was more than an inch deep in dead and dying ants.

For most of us ants are a bit of a nuisance: they sometimes get into the kitchen and become a pest; they fly on hot summer evenings and, attracted to the lights, leave a mass of now superfluous wings on the carpet; and sometimes they give painful bites and stings. But there is more to ants than this. For one thing there are thousands of different sorts of ant, quite as different from one another as we are from baboons and bush-babies. Some in the tropics are large with exceedingly painful stings; others are minute but live in colonies of hundreds of thousands. Many are predatory and kill and eat caterpillars and other insects. Most notorious are the army and driver ants of tropical Africa and America which bivouac for a few weeks in a hole in the ground or in a hollow tree base and then march over a broad front killing every living thing they encounter with their enormous sickle-like jaws in order to feed their developing brood. One tragic night in Ghana driver ants passed through the University Zoology Department where I worked, and found a cage containing a two metre long spitting cobra. When we arrived in the morning there was just a skeleton and a few strands of meat remaining of the poor creature; its potent venom was useless against these deadly insects. Then there are harvester ants which collect and feed on plant seeds, honeypot ants some of whose workers have hugely distended abdomens full of honey for the entire colony to eat, and leafcutter ants of the Americas which cultivate fungi to extract nutrients from the leaves they collect, and then the ants eat the fungi.

Most of these ants live in large colonies with workers, soldiers, kings (usually short-lived) and queens. The queen founded the colony and is the sole egg layer. All of the workers and soldiers are infertile females, and just once a year they rear broods of larger ants which develop wings, the flying kings and queens. The behaviour of the colony is exceedingly complex with elaborate communication by means of touch and chemicals (pheromones). The workers and soldiers spend their entire lives in the service of the colony, even defending it to the death. Such sacrifice is unusual in the animal world where selfishness is more the norm. But it is not really altruism: if you cannot yourself reproduce, the best way to propagate your own genes is to help your sisters, each of whom shares half of your genes. Nevertheless the industry and selfless devotion to the common good make ants a model for our own society. Never mind that ants seem to act almost 100% instinctively with no trace of conscious thought: they are by and large a remarkably successful group of animals judged by their incredible diversity and enormous numbers, particularly in the tropics where every plant seems to be overrun by ants of one sort or another.

Our own society, by contrast, seems to be aiming for less work and more rewards for the individual, rather than for society as a whole. We have hospitals and welfare services, and the people who work there support the community, but the overall aim of our society at present seems to be to enable everyone to develop their own aspirations, even if some of these are to the detriment of others. Yet if ants can strive for the common good with, as far as we can see, no conscious thought whatever, surely we with our elaborate brains and remarkable methods of communication should be able to do much, much better?

Contemporary slave raiders

Amongst the thousands of species of ants in the world with remarkably diverse ways of making a living, are some that parallel ourselves in carrying out slave-raids and then keeping the slaves captive to look after themselves. We have about fifty different species of ants in Britain, nothing like as diverse in habits as tropical ants, but with some fascinating variations in behaviour nonetheless.

Most ants are omnivorous like ourselves, taking both animal and vegetable food. They search for small insects, woodlice and other arthropods which they kill and take back to the nest, and a few species take the sugary nectar produced in special organs (called extrafloral nectaries) by plants such as vetches and bracken. The plant benefits from providing this food because the ants run all over it searching for the nectar and will kill or chase off any caterpillar or other insect they find which might eat the plant. However, the commonest vegetable food for British ants is actually processed first by aphids (greenfly, blackfly and their relatives). Aphids suck up sugar-water from the conducting tissues of plants, and because essential amino-acids are scarce in this tissue, they have to imbibe a large quantity of sugary liquid to extract them. Surplus sugar-water accumulates as droplets near the anus which are then eaten by ants. Both animals benefit from this relationship: the ant gets nourishment while the aphid gets rid of waste sugars and is protected from predatory insects by the ants which guard them carefully.

The ants that we normally see are sterile female workers, but the colonies rear winged males and females during the summer months. During the nuptial flight these kings and queens mate, and then comes the most dangerous task of all for the queen, founding a new colony. It is dangerous because to begin with she has no workers to help her lay eggs, find food, and look after the young until they grow to adult workers capable of defending the colony and foraging for food. It only needs one predatory insect to find her at that time and she and her brood can all be killed. Later when she has hundreds of worker and soldier daughters, the colony is far less vulnerable to attack by other insects.

One way of overcoming this vulnerable period is sometimes used by the red wood-ant (*Formica rufa*) whose nests comprise large mounds of pine needles. The mated queen searches out the nest of a weaker, black species of ant, kills the queen, and then takes over the nest using the surviving workers to look after her own eggs and her own brood until eventually they die leaving only her own offspring. This strategy does not always succeed – sometimes the workers of the host colony kill her because she does not have the right chemical signals, but evidently for some ants this is a safer way of founding a new colony than attempting it single-handed.

The red slave-raider ant (*Formica sanguinea*), which is widespread in the south of Britain but less common further north, has rather different habits. The workers are large with powerful jaws and painful stings, and they invade colonies of smaller black ants (*Formica fusca*), kill any opposition, and steal the pupae (the so-called ant eggs) which they take to their own colony. These hatch out, forage and look after the colony of their slave-raider hosts until they die. The slave-raiders care for them, probably more effectively than their own colony can because they are larger with more painful stings. Our British red slave-raiding ants can live a normal colony life with their own workers carrying out all the necessary duties, but very often they use slaves to do their work instead. Some other slave-raiders cannot survive without slaves.

We humans have our own parasites and exploiters, people who live off the work of others and do little for themselves. And there are still far too many parts of the world where servants are effectively slaves and where children are exploited. The difference between us and the ants is that they act almost entirely by instinct, so for them there is no 'right' and 'wrong' behaviour. Most people have an ethical code that tells us to care for other human beings, so such overt exploitation should not be tolerated. But it is tolerated, partly because it can be dressed up as 'providing work and a livelihood for someone who would otherwise have none'. However, the ant situation also differs in that the slaves belong to a different species, as different from the slavemakers as we are from monkeys and elephants. So the parallel is really with ourselves exploiting other animals as our own slaves. Animals in zoos, and monkeys and chimpanzees for medical and scientific research are good examples – can we really justify these activities? Cattle, sheep and dogs are slightly different because they have taken thousands of generations to produce the breeds alive today, and, unlike cats, many could not possibly survive without

help from people. Yet, even with this long history of domestication and adaptation to ourselves, we can still ask is it ethically acceptable to keep such animals, and if so, how should they be kept?

~

Pax Argentinica

Argentina spans such a diversity of latitudes and habitats that it has more than 500 different species of ant, compared with fewer than 50 in Britain, but there is one small species which is commonly called the Argentine ant. The Argentine ant (*Iridomyrmex humilis*) thrives in a warm climate with hot dry summers and it lives, like many other species of ant, in large colonies. The workers, all sterile sisters, forage widely collecting food for the colony. They can recognise members of their own colony by their characteristic scent and these they greet in typical ant-fashion. But workers from neighbouring colonies are attacked. Such skirmishes range from brief attack and retreat to mass warfare, with hundreds or thousands on either side being called up as reinforcements (by means of scent signals) to drive the enemy off. Such battles can result in the deaths of thousands of ants and leave both colonies severely weakened.

So the Argentine ant in its native home behaves very like any other species of ant. However, it is a successful traveller and has used ships or aeroplanes to colonise parts of California and the Mediterranean which have a similar climate to Argentina. In its new homes the Argentine ant has to fight off other species of ant (just as it does in Argentina), but its behaviour towards neighbouring colonies of its own species is quite different. Instead of fighting neighbours viciously, these Argentine ants greet them peaceably, and if there is a threat from a different species of local ant then they will recruit not only their own colony members but also Argentine ants from neighbouring colonies in their defence. Instead of living in small, mutually exclusive colonies they live in a very large area with several colony centres, and any ant is free to take refuge in any of these centres. The result is that these invasive Argentine ants have become very successful indeed in their new homes.

The parallel with ourselves is remarkable. For most of human history we have lived in small communities, mistrusting most of our neighbours and often in conflict or even warfare with them. The most successful human societies have followed the example of the Argentine ants: the Roman empire at its height gave many of its conquered peoples full rights of citizenship so that they supported the empire because it gave them a security lacking in smaller discrete groups. Today we see even more cooperation along these lines with cities and towns grouped into nations and these linked by treaties of peace and cooperation – the European Economic Community and NATO are obvious examples. There is even an attempt to encompass the whole world in this grouping (the United Nations), but it tends to be a theoretical ideal rather than a reality. Opposed to this movement are the more extreme forms of national identity in which neighbours of different ethnic or religious natures are persecuted, as in the balkans, Israel and Afghanistan.

How do the Argentine ants achieve this transformation to an allegiance towards the entire species in their new homes? The answer lies in their genes because the genes determine colony odour. Ants treat sisters from their own colony as friends because they recognise their smell, while ants from elsewhere are treated as enemies because they have a different colony smell. Because the colonies in California were founded by just one or a few ants the different colonies here are genetically much more uniform than ant colonies back in Argentina, and so neighbouring ants are recognised as sisters. Careful research has shown that a few colonies back in Argentina whose queens are closely related do not attack each other, while some of the long established and distant colonies in California behave aggressively to each other. Nevertheless, if animals with such minute brains as ants can take the enormous step from allegiance only to close relatives to

 allegiance to all neighbours of the same species, then surely we humans, with our highly developed powers of reason, should also be able to treat other humans in the same way as we treat our brothers and sisters?

~

Wasps

Wasps are almost everyone's least liked insect, because they have a passion for getting into raspberry jam and because they sting if unduly provoked. But they have plenty of admirable qualities as well.

Like bumblebees, only mated queen wasps survive the winter, and these can often be found clinging to curtains in cool underused rooms or in dry outhouses. Then as the spring sunshine warms the air they become active, feed on nectar, and start to build a papier-maché nest from finely stripped wood (often from wooden window frames) macerated with saliva. The nest may be in a hole in the ground or in a hedge or attic, depending on the species of wasp – we have half a dozen species of wasp (*Vespula vulgaris* and related species) in Britain, all very similar in appearance but differing in colour and pattern of markings on the face and antennae as well as in their habits. Inside the nest they build cells and lay an egg in each one. The grubs are fed on chewed up insects, mainly flies and caterpillars, and the first generation of young to emerge are all sterile workers. For the rest of the summer these and subsequent broods of sterile workers do all the work: enlarging the nest, building cells and stocking them with chewed up food for the young. All the queen has to do is lay eggs and accept whatever food her daughters give her. A colony destroys an enormous number of insects including house flies, blue-bottles and many caterpillars which are pests of garden plants, so wasps should really be our friends, just as are honeybees and bumblebees.

But wasps also have a fondness for jam and other sugary foods, so when we decide the weather is warm enough to eat outside they are attracted by the smell and come to join the feast. In late summer the now elderly queen produces a brood of fertile males and females after which she is exhausted and eventually dies. Her enormous family of daughters now have little left to do.

They may continue to rear a few more young but many simply spend their time searching for sugary food, and if it is somewhat fermented so much the better. These are now the lager louts of the insect world: if disturbed they buzz or fly drunkenly around and they may sting at the slightest provocation. A few score wasps and green- and blue-bottle flies can soon make inroads on a crop of plums or autumn raspberries, often doing so before the fruit is fully ripe. No wonder we dislike them.

Come to think of it, wasps are not really so very different from ourselves. Many of us are industrious and hard-working, serving our community well for much of our lives. But others take to excessive drinking or go on drugs, and some may become physically violent on the least provocation. And as with the drunken wasps we try to avoid such people if we possibly can. The wasp society can afford to degenerate in the autumn, because all of the old ones are going to die anyway before spring, and then a new industrious community will start all over again. In contrast our society continues throughout the year, so these social misfits can become a burden on society, and we have to work at trying to prevent people from developing antisocial behaviour.

~

How doth the little Busy Bee?

If I want to tell you about a good shop where you can buy ice cream (or corsets for that matter) I can give you precise directions: go into town, straight over at the first set of lights, turn right at the second lights into Winckley Street, and it is the fourth shop on your left. And with any luck you should find it without any problem. But try communicating this information to one of our closest relatives, a chimpanzee or a bonobo, and you will run into problems. Substitute bananas for ice cream, because they love eating bananas, and there will still be a problem. Partly it is a matter of language, but chimpanzees are quite unable to communicate similar directions to fellow chimpanzees, not even a 'go past the large baobab tree and after about 20 seconds and slightly to your left there is a super fig tree'. Indeed there is no evidence that any mammal or bird can give directions to a friend on how to find a specific site. Among vertebrates this appears to be a uniquely human attribute. Is this because we alone among animals have a complex language?

Well, no, a complex language is not necessary in order to give precise directions to a friend, and there is one animal that can do this very effectively indeed: the honeybee (*Apis mellifera*). If a worker bee finds a new rich source of nectar, on its return to the hive it performs a simple dance which communicates this information to fellow bees. If the nectar was fairly close, up to 100 metres away, then it performs a round dance on the vertical surface of the honeycomb. The bees which closely follow the dancing bee pick up the scent of the nectar from the dancer and fly off searching in all directions until they find it. But if the nectar was much further away, a kilometre perhaps, then the returning bee performs a waggle dance. Again the following bees pick up the scent of the plant but they all fly off in precisely the right direction for the right distance in order to find the nectar. How do they know the direction and the distance? Well, the waggle dance follows a figure of 8 on its side (the symbol for infinity, ∞) in which the central vertical part of the dance (between the left and right loops) represents the direction of the sun. If the food source is 20^0 to the right of the sun then this vertical part of the dance will be angled 20^0 to the right of the vertical, and the number of times the abdomen is waggled from side to side during this part of the dance gives information on the distance from the hive. This is the so-called language of the bees, first discovered by Karl von Frisch (for which he was awarded the Nobel Prize).

So bees can perform a feat that is beyond the capability of any other animal, vertebrate or invertebrate, apart from ourselves. Does this mean they have intelligence or conscious thought comparable with that of humans? Not really; the waggle dance is not a language, it gives only three pieces of information, and none of the information is constructed into sentences. The bee's brain is smaller than a pin-head, and there is no evidence that bees have a brain, sensory and motor nervous system any more complex than that of a fly, indeed it is questionable whether they can even feel pain in the sense that we can think "ouch that really hurts". They can respond to being attacked (by stinging or trying to fly away) just as they respond to a variety of other stimuli. But as for possessing higher faculties of the brain such as those of great apes or dolphins, no, their brain is no more complex than that of many other insects. Does this mean that other insects can also transmit information to their fellows? Not necessarily; what it tells us is that the sensory and neural systems of insects are sufficiently complex for such remarkable behaviour to evolve, but it will only evolve if the environment is such that it is advantageous (in terms of eggs laid or offspring produced) to do so. It would be of no benefit whatsoever to non-social insects like flies or butterflies, so of course it has not evolved in them. Evolution by means of natural selection which has produced such complex behaviour in such a simple animal as a bee really is the most remarkable wonder of the natural world.

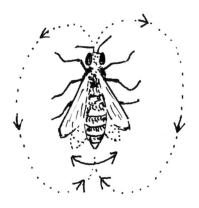

CHAPTER 3

Primates

Delinquent Chimps

Many readers will have seen TV programmes on Jane Goodall's twenty-five years' study of the chimpanzees in the Gombe Nature Reserve in Tanzania. Her book *In the Shadow of Man* described the early years of this work, including her fascinating discovery of chimpanzees' tool use and the tragic results of a polio epidemic. Less well known is her account in the *National Geographic Magazine* in 1979, which demonstrated that the longer the study continued the more interesting and profound are the insights it gives into how chimp society works, and of how this resembles and differs from human society. Two incidents were, to me, particularly disturbing.

First there was the chimp called Passion. She appeared to be a normal adult female until one day she was observed to attack another female, Gilka, and to kill her baby. Later Passion and her adolescent daughter Pom killed and ate several other baby chimps, the combined force of mother and daughter being too much for most of the females to be able to protect their babies. Assuming that some babies that mysteriously disappeared at this time were also killed, it seems that Passion probably killed as many as ten baby chimps in this way. No other female chimps behaved like this during twenty-five years of study, and when Passion died the habit died with her: Pom did not continue it on her own.

The second incident occurred when the troupe of fifty or so chimps became so large that it split into two groups. Chimpanzees usually have close and friendly relationships within their group. There is a dominance hierarchy among the males, but disputes are more often settled by displays (including a terrifying charge) than by overt violence. However, after the split, patrols of males from the larger group were several times seen to attack solitary males from the smaller group. These were not merely attacks to assert dominance: they were so vicious that five males were so badly injured that they died. Eventually the smaller troupe had no adult males left and it then merged with the larger group.

It is sometimes misleading to draw too close comparisons between behaviour in humans and in other animals but, as Jane Goodall commented, the frightening thing is not how different chimpanzees are from humans, but how similar. Delinquents like Passion occur in human society for no apparent reason. It is difficult to see how infanticide can be of advantage to a society since if the habit were to spread the population would die out. It is also difficult to see how it could benefit Passion's own genes: there was no evidence that Passion's young were threatened in any way by the other baby chimps in the group. One would like to know what Passion's own family background was like and what made her go off the rails, but unfortunately she was already adult when the study began.

The "mugging" or gang warfare among males is also very similar to human behaviour, but here there was a biological advantage: it resulted in adding more females to the group and so it increased the chances that these males would mate and father more young.

Are we any better than the Gombe chimps? Socially destructive behaviour, murder and mugging occur in human society as well. The only real difference is that we can recognise the behaviour in others, talk about it, and take carefully planned action to try to prevent it from occurring again. Yet if we look at the world around us we have to ask very seriously whether we are actually doing enough.

~

Our aggression and its Animal Origins

Two letters in *The Friend* of September 2nd 1988 alluded to natural behaviour of humans as having evolved; but the types of behaviour the writers considered "natural" appear to be contradictory. Victor Oubridge wrote: "The evolutionary factors, even for and within the human race itself, have been aggression, competition and the vanquishing of one's opponents", and: "The reverence for life which is hesitatingly emerging leads us to reject the amoral life of the jungle and with it the competitive instincts which, nevertheless, have brought us to where we are". John Lenthall says: "Looking at our natural origins, I think that we may see our regard for good – our sense that our behaviour should be helpful, or at least not harmful, to our fellows – traces back to the instincts which all creatures have, to behave in ways that are good for the species".

I think that it would be helpful to take a closer look at the behaviour of other species and to see how our own behaviour compares with theirs. In this way we can get some idea about how much of our aggressive and co-operative behaviour we have inherited from our pre-human ancestors, and what may be considered uniquely human.

Many animals show aggressiveness, and quite a few have co-operative behaviour. Aggressive encounters occur both between animals of different species and within a species, but here I am just considering the latter. The aggressive behaviour, in biological terminology, is not confined to fighting, but includes a variety of looks, gestures, and ritualised behaviours that are intended to intimidate a rival. In this context it is better to use the term "agonistic behaviour".

In other animals there is a relation between both agonistic and co-operative behaviours and the degree of gregariousness. At one extreme there are entirely solitary species, whose only contact with others is for a brief period of mating, and in the case of mammals, birds and some other groups, while the mother is caring for young. Such animals usually maintain some form of territory, though in some species these may overlap; and some animals are nomadic wanderers that avoid others but hold no territory. Those with a territory will defend it from other individuals, though this may not involve contact. Large cats such as leopards scent-mark the boundaries of their territories, which others respect. This spaces them out so that resources are not over-utilised.

At the other extreme there are vast shoals, flocks or herds as in some fish, birds and antelope (like the wildebeest on the Serengeti Plains). Such groups have virtually no internal structure; each animal has the same relation to any other, there is no hierarchy, though in several species an individual has a "personal space" from which it excludes others, so there is little physical touching. These groups do not normally hold territories.

Between these extremes are animals that form smaller structured groups, with particular individual relations within the group. Most such groups live in a territory. The groups may be based on a nuclear family or be larger, with most related as an extended family or clan, though the males have often come in from outside. The family normally lives in and defends a territory against rival groups, though as with solitary animals this need not involve conflict. The function of defending a territory is the same as in solitary species. If the populations increase, or if there are other pressures on resources, agonistic behaviour is likely to take more severe forms including fighting. Fighting is most likely the closer the opponents are matched. The object of fighting, as of all agonistic behaviour, is to keep the opponents out of the territory, or to drive out a territory occupant in order to acquire a territory; it is not normally to kill, though sometimes an animal may die of its wounds. Killing has occasionally been observed in territorial fights – in captive rats it occurs if the vanquished rat cannot escape. It has been seen occasionally in hyaenas. In Jane Goodall's study of chimpanzees there was one group which split from another, and after a while the males of the original group systematically killed a large proportion of the splinter group. One does not know if in this case there were additional factors, such as human activities, preventing the splinter group from moving away as far as it might normally do, but this was the only time such killing was seen in twenty-five years.

Structured Groups

In species that live in structured groups, agonistic behaviour also occurs within the group. In this case it is normally employed towards creating and maintaining a hierarchical structure or "peck order". If the group is stable, then the intensity of the behaviour may be low: a look could be sufficient to make a subordinate back away from a dominant who wants the food or best resting place. However, if a dominant is being challenged by an up-and-coming individual, fights can occur. Again these seldom result in death and, depending on the group structure, the ex-dominant may eventually take a subordinate place, leave the group, or relinquish a harem of females. Killing occurs occasionally. When a male lion takes over a pride it kills small cubs fathered by the vanquished male which brings the lionesses into heat shortly after. As the tenure of a pride is normally only about two years, this action will significantly increase the number of offspring the male will father. Infanticide occurs in a few other species with a similar lifestyle. There is some evidence that baboons which have to defend themselves from leopards have a higher level of agonistic behaviour than those groups that do not. Animals with structured groups show an increase in agonistic behaviour with increase in the size of the group. This is not just due to increased pressure on resources; if food supply is maintained it still occurs if groups get too large. It appears that most individuals have a limit to the number of their kind they can recognise, and as this is stretched group members are treated as outsiders and the group's structure breaks down

Families and clans

There are other lifestyles, but those described here are the commonest. Most primates, to which humans belong, live in either nuclear family groups or larger clans. Our closest relatives, the chimpanzees, have the latter, and so probably did the common ancestor from which we both evolved.

However, co-operation between individuals is another characteristic behaviour of animals living in groups. In lions and chimps two males may co-operate to overcome, or at least avoid being bullied by, the dominant. Defending territory against rival groups, defending the group against predators, and communal hunting can all involve co-operation. Caring for young occurs in many species: in most cats and primates it is just by the mother, in jackals by both sexes, in wolves and African hunting dogs by all of the pack. Offspring learn skills from their parents in many animals.

So proto-humans would have shown agonistic behaviour, both within their group and against other groups, but also co-operation within the group. The amount of overt aggression there would have been is difficult to assess. In the early days, with a sparse population, pressure on resources may have been light and so any competition between groups could be dealt with by spacing out and colonising new areas, Within the group, behaviour would have probably been similar to present-day chimps, with some aggression that varied with individuals, which was probably only severe when an up-and-coming young male wished to challenge an old dominant. During the time since chimps separated from a chimp-human ancestor, there has been more than one species of early hominid. All were making and using tools (which chimps can also do in a simple way), and evolving larger brains and so presumably more complex thought processes. It is the development of our ability to use tools, to work out ideas, and a spiritual and moral sense that separates us from other living animals. I would not like to speculate on the degree of development of intelligence and moral thought in other early hominids.

Our use of tools and our intelligence have taken us beyond other animals in the extent of both our agonistic and our co-operative behaviour. They allow us to kill other groups and to terrorise within the group in a way that no other animal does. It is important to remember that our agonistic behaviour has its roots in our pre-human evolution, but extreme development seems to be a speciality of our species.

However, we have also evolved communal activities, from hunting, tilling the earth, and building to enjoying ourselves in a way that no other animal has. Unlike other communal animals, such as ants, our co-operation is endlessly adaptable to the circumstances, if we wish it to be. This is where our third special attribute comes in: we can use our spiritual and moral sense to utilise our intelligence and technological abilities to find ways of lessening the excesses of our aggressive behaviour. The need to do this is ever more pressing, for one of the factors that makes agonistic behaviour more aggressive is pressure on resources. And now the pressures are increasing at an alarming rate by our profligate use of limited resources. So as well as remembering that our behaviour has roots in our evolutionary past, we need also to remember that our ecology does as well, that our resources are only this planet, and that these are not unlimited.

Janet Edmunds

~

Behaving like a Baboon

Monkeys and apes have a fascination for us, perhaps because they seem to reflect a part of ourselves. Baby monkeys and apes are especially attractive because of their similarity to human babies. But baboons are, to my mind at any rate, among the least attractive of the monkeys: their long snout and large canine teeth give them more of a resemblance to a dog or a wolf than to a monkey, so they are far less cuddly, and the enormous males have a reputation for tremendous fighting ability. Indeed with their huge canines, high-crowned head and powerful muscular build, they are superbly designed fighting machines. The big males dominate the troupe and the biggest get to the top by sheer fighting power.

Such was the received wisdom when Shirley Strum began a study of baboons in Kenya in 1972. She started by breaking all the rules: baboons are dangerous animals so never leave your Land-Rover when they are near. But she soon found that the best way to study them was to sit quietly in the middle of the troupe which quickly got used to her and then ignored her completely.

There certainly was aggression in the colony, but usually these instances were settled by displays or a brief chase, and actual physical fighting was very rare. Combat was particularly rare among the males, probably because fighting could be very damaging even to the winner who would actually gain very little from the effort. One strategy used by a baboon (of either sex) when threatened by a larger one is to seize a small juvenile and hold this in front of them to inhibit the aggressor. Large baboons are reluctant to attack babies. Threatened males will also quickly find a female with whom they are friendly and begin to groom her. This also halts pursuing males.

Even more surprising was the behaviour of young males when they left their natal troupe. Females normally live their entire lives in the troupe in which they are born, but males typically move out to join another troupe when sexually mature. The old view was that, like lions, they have to fight their way into a new troupe by defeating the top ranking male in battle, but this proved to be a myth. The young male trying to enter a new troupe would spend most of his time at the edge of the group. As soon as he moved towards one of the residents they would flee – even the biggest male would retreat as he approached, or else find a female to groom and then ignore the intruder. So the newest males get the best feeding and sleeping places, and they do this without fighting. But this is all they have: they do not get to mate because the females all flee from strange males. However, over a period of a year or eighteen months the new male persists in approaching one or two females or juveniles in the troupe until they accept him. It takes three years for him to be fully integrated into the group so that he can then consort and mate with females and play a full part in the life of the troupe, but by then he is no longer the feared intruder. In his relations with other males he remains less at ease than with females or young, but he has become one of the group. Social interactions and good relationships with others count for much more than brute force and strength in achieving success in baboon society.

Baboons are essentially monkeys of the savanna and their way of life is not so different from what we think life must have been like for early humans in the savannas of East Africa. The parallels are clear. In ourselves too the male is much more of a fighting animal than the female, and although men lack obvious anatomical weapons they make ever more powerful and lethal weapons for fighting. But fighting prowess does not necessarily lead to reproductive success or we would have evolved much more pronounced physical differences between the sexes. No, success goes to the shrewd, the clever, the manipulators, the ones who can create coalitions, just as it does in baboon society, and the best way of creating an alliance is by social grooming or other interactions which in humans we call friendship. So Shirley Strum calls her book about her work *Almost Human*, but perhaps it would be truer to say that it is *we* who are very like baboons in our social behaviour and interactions with other people.

~

Human origins

I was interested to read the commentary in *The Friend* of 15th March 1991 about Sir Alister Hardy's theory of the aquatic origin of humans. I do not know the more recent books by Elaine Morgan (referred to there), but readers may be interested to hear how Alister Hardy's original ideas came about. When his article appeared in *New Scientist* in 1960 he was already close to retirement after a long spell as Professor of Zoology at Oxford University, but nobody at Oxford at that time was quite sure if he was serious about his theory or not. It must have been in 1959 that he was invited to give an after dinner talk to the British Sub-Aqua Club and it was here that he first outlined his theory of our descent from an aquatic ancestor. He had a keen sense of humour and would have revelled in the opportunity to propose an outlandish theory on such an occasion. But the press were there and immediately picked it up, hence the invitation to write an article for *New Scientist*. He gave a seminar on his theory at Oxford where he explained that he had no idea that the press would report his talk, but he also admitted that he felt there might after all be something other than pure spoof in his theory.

When his first grandchild was born he very much wanted to fill the bath full and see if the infant would naturally float, but he wasn't sure how the baby's parents would react to it! We never knew if he really took his idea seriously but one of the staff found a poem lying around which was believed to have been coined by Bernard Kettlewell (who carried out classic experiments on the industrial melanic peppered moth). It went, as far as I can recall, thus:

> Oh mistress mine when I do find
> How softly feel thy buttocks,
> I close my eyes and do surmise
> That they were once aquatics.
> So if you find that your behind
> Gets fatter than it oughter,
> With joy recall, you'll need it all
> When we return to water.

As to the final point in the commentary, and Hardy's views on God, he published two volumes in the 1960s: *The Living Stream* which is mainly the biological basis of evolution, and *The Divine Flame* which looks at our relationship with God.

~

On Being Human

In David Attenborough's superb *Trials of Life* there is a remarkable sequence of chimpanzees from Côte d'Ivoire hunting colobus monkeys. This was not a casual, opportunistic occurrence, as it is with Jane Goodall's chimps at Gombe in Tanzania where the males occasionally kill young baboons. No, in Côte d'Ivoire chimps it is a daily happening at certain times of the year, and it involves close co-operation between half a dozen or more animals, with even more precise coordination than occurs with a hunting pride of lions. What happens is that the group of chimps moves over the forest floor with eyes facing upwards, alert for any movement in the canopy above. When they see a group of monkeys their behaviour changes. The monkeys in turn usually see them and begin to move away. Some chimps follow on the ground but a few nip quickly up carefully chosen trees so that they can drive the monkeys in one particular direction. Eventually the monkeys find themselves surrounded by chimps on the ground or in medium sized trees, so they move up into the biggest trees. Then one chimp follows them up and this causes them to panic. Some may try to leap into a neighbouring tree only to be grabbed by a waiting chimp, while others try to get past the pursuing giant. Many escape, but often one is caught and quite simply torn limb from limb by the chimps. They eat some of the monkey and then carry the carcass down to share with the rest of the troupe.

Some viewers found the sequence disturbing, bloodthirsty, and altogether not very nice viewing, perhaps because of the closeness of chimpanzees to humans. One response is to denigrate chimps, as Libby Purves did on Radio 4 when she referred to them as David Attenborough's 'horrid little monkeys'. This is the same as the attitude encouraged in human armies, of dehumanising the enemy so as to destroy any inhibitions about killing fellow humans. Monkeys differ from us in appearance and behaviour, so something they do can be regarded as horrid, beneath our own human dignity and behaviour. But of course, chimpanzees are not monkeys, they are apes, and apes have far more similarities to ourselves than they do to any of the monkeys. Indeed the animal that is most similar to a chimpanzee in its genes and its behaviour is not the gorilla nor even the orang-utan, but ourselves: over 98% of our genes are shared with chimpanzees*. So what we see in chimps is very often a reflection of what we can see in ourselves, if we care to look.

Look at the delight taken by hunt followers at the kill of a fox, and the practice of blooding children with its blood, or the glee in the faces of spectators at a bull fight when the tormented animal is tortured to death, or even the crowd at a boxing match baying for one or other contestant to be physically hurt and for blood to flow. But that is *other* people, not us. Yet if we were desperately short of protein would we too be prepared to kill a chicken or a sheep with our bare hands? Most of us feel there is something not quite nice about killing animals: why else do we insist on keeping it hidden in an abattoir? In my own profession (I am a lecturer in biology) we do the same: if a rat or a frog is to be killed it is done humanely but discreetly so as not to upset people's feelings.

Killing and love of blood *is* part of the human condition, but so too is the revulsion and the feeling that this is somehow 'wrong'. There is much to be commended in the American Indian's attitude to animals: yes they do have to be killed sometimes, but they deserve our deepest respect. It is this reverence for the lives of other animals that seems to be so lacking in many aspects of human behaviour today. 'Inasmuch as ye have done it unto one of the least of these my brethren, ye have done it unto me.'

~

---

* not strictly correct: we share 98% of or genes with both the chimpanzee and the closely related bonobo.

Thirty Years with Chimpanzees

The first ten years of Jane Goodall's study of the chimpanzees of Gombe in Tanzania was described in a delightful book *In the Shadow of Man*. Her second book on the lives and deaths of these chimps, *The Chimpanzees of Gombe* (1986), brings the study to a staggering thirty years. Jane Goodall and her team of research students have seen an entire generation of chimpanzees from birth to maturity, old age and death. They know all the bonds of relationship, friendship and group loyalty and can attempt to interpret the fascinating behavioural interrelationships between all the different individuals, each of which is as different in temperament and character as are the people living in a street. The life of a male chimp is very often a striving for dominance, and while power and strength are important in rising to become alpha male (because they have to fight), it is surprising how often other qualities prove to be more important than sheer strength. Having a brother to help in fights is one way of rising up the hierarchy, but another is to form a liaison or friendship with an unrelated male, or indeed with the current alpha male. And even more important is to have a dramatic charging display to intimidate rivals. Sheer determination to win can enable a male of only moderate size to rise to the top.

In the females there is also a pecking order, but it is far less important to the social life of a female than it is for a male. Much more important are bonds of kinship and other non-family social ties. Females develop lasting bonds with all their children which help sustain them when they get old, and they create genuine friendships with other adults of both sexes. Sex itself appeared at first to be a largely communal affair with females accepting almost any male during her oestrus, but this is probably not the usual situation. At the start of a female's oestrus a male will do his utmost to lure her away to a remote part of the colony's range where other chimps rarely go. This can be by mutual agreement, or he can beat her until she reluctantly follows him on their 'honeymoon'. Once away the female is literally lost and so must stay with the male until he decides to return to familiar landmarks, and by then she is no longer attractive to other males. Nevertheless, in spite of this behaviour, it seems likely that the dominant males father most of the young, in the same way that they do in most other social mammals that have been studied.

Jane Goodall describes in detail the splitting of the group into two and the subsequent 'gang warfare' between these groups with the larger eventually attacking and killing all of the adult males of the smaller group. This, and the delinquent female, Passion, who developed the habit of stealing the young of other females and then killing and eating them, has already been outlined in my article on delinquent chimps. The book also describes the cruelty shown by others to a deposed, but now weak, leader and to a formerly high-ranking female in her decrepit old age. But to set against these less pleasant attributes there are outstanding instances of compassion (love?) between mother and child or between a young chimp and his or her mother. Sometimes a mother dies and her adolescent daughter does her utmost to look after the baby sister or brother. There are even instances of altruism between quite unrelated individuals, something that is not often found in the non-human world of animals. In fact the longer the study goes on the closer do chimps appear to be to ourselves, and it is possible to see human parallels in almost every aspect of their behaviour. How tragic then to report on the shrinking of the forest home of Africa's chimps. The book ends by examining the culture of this our closest relative throughout Africa, partly because the forests are being cut to give us more hardwood doors and sideboards (and also land for peasants to farm), and partly because it pays hunters to shoot mother chimps with babies: the babies can be sold to middlemen and eventually end up with beach photographers on the Costa del Sol or in a laboratory for Aids or hepatitis research. What an appalling abuse of medical research to confine an animal that shares more than 98% of its genes with ourselves in a cage with no companions or things to do, and then to give it one of the most horrible of human diseases.

~

Monkey business

An adult male chimpanzee has decided to challenge the next male above him in the hierarchy. To begin with the two scream and display, charging around, tearing up saplings and hurling branches and rocks. Then, since neither backs off, they fight with teeth and fingernails, but only briefly before one decides he cannot win, and makes off. Half an hour later the two are together again, but this time after accepting the submission of the loser, the winner embraces his former opponent and they groom each other.

Of course not all such incidents end quite so quickly. Sometimes the two combatants sit a few yards apart glaring and bristling with hostility. And then a female comes up to one and grooms him in such a way that he is clearly expected to groom her in return. Once he has started to do so she moves slowly towards the other male with her consort following, still grooming. Eventually she grooms the second male, and he reciprocates, so she receives attention from both males, and then quietly slips away leaving them surprised to find themselves grooming each other.

'Reconciliation', 'conflict resolution' and 'mediation' are words that were rarely used a generation ago, but in recent years a complete discipline has developed in this area such that there are now people in many parts of Britain and the world who are involved in these activities and who try to pass on their skills to others. For those of us who sit on the sidelines and admire this development, there is a tendency to think of mediation as being a recently developed skill, something that was either absent in past centuries, or at least not a quality that was valued by society.

However, there have always been people who were skilled in conflict resolution and mediation, even though these were very much a last resort in the face of likely defeat; the 'glories' of war seemed much more important. But, in fact, these skills are much older than *Homo sapiens.* They occur not only in our closest relatives, the chimpanzees, but also in many species of monkey.

Male chimpanzees and social monkeys strive for dominance and inevitably this involves fighting. But fighting can be damaging and disrupts the colony by putting it at greater risk of danger from predators. Unlike in lions, where the defeated pride male is banished, primate societies cannot afford to lose defeated males who are still valuable in protecting the colony. So in rhesus monkeys, baboons, chimpanzees and bonobos, males who have fought often 'make up' not long afterwards.

Reconciliation after a fight is almost invariable in males in captive colonies, but does not occur so often in the less aggressive females or in wild colonies. In a natural colony the vanquished combatant can avoid meeting the victor and so there is little advantage to be gained by reconciliation. But where they are likely to meet frequently it will benefit them both if they can make peace and get on with their everyday lives without worrying about a possible further conflict.

The method of reconciliation varies in different species: chimps do it with a kiss on the mouth, golden monkeys by holding hands, but the result is the same: the two individuals then go about their everyday business.

Mediators in chimpanzee and other primate societies are often the dominant males. When a fight breaks out between two lower ranking males or between two females, the dominant male sometimes wades in and separates the combatants. Sometimes when others have joined in, he will beat them indiscriminately (without taking sides) until they stop and the colony regains its normal composure. Mediation from a position of dominance is widespread in human societies also: disputes are often submitted to the king or chief who has to adjudicate, and usually the decision is accepted.

But mediation can also be carried out by lower-ranking individuals, as shown by the female chimpanzee already described. A female chimpanzee can also mediate before a fight: sometimes when two males are displaying and threatening each other with screams and weapons, she can move up to one and remove the rock from his hand. The situation is defused and the two males lose interest.

Can the skills of reconciliation and mediation be learned? Some years ago the Dutch ethologist Frans de Waal carried out an experiment using captive rhesus and stump-tail macaque monkeys. Rhesus monkeys are very easily provoked to violence and often do not make peace after a fight, whereas the larger stump-tails are more laid back, often ignore provocation, and soon reconcile after a dispute. Waal put a small captive colony of each species together in the same enclosure. At first the rhesus monkeys were scared of the larger stump-tails, but soon learned that there was nothing to fear and behaved much as they would on their own, but with one important difference: they fought much less, but when they did, they made peace much more frequently. This change in behaviour occurred even though the two species reconcile by using quite different behaviours, and it persisted for several weeks after the rhesus monkeys were separated from the stump-tails.

Can we learn anything useful about reconciliation and mediation from the behaviour of other primates? Children can reconcile after a fight and become good friends, but all too often people, both as individuals and in groups, prefer to hold grudges and seek revenge. The primate society in which a defeated male becomes an outcast is weaker by one powerful male, and so it may not be able to withstand a challenge from a neighbouring group trying to extend its territory, or to ward off attacks from leopards or other predators.

Human societies today lack this immediate pressure to reconcile and maximise the strength of the group. Perhaps we need the threat of some outside group to make us see the need to reconcile? Margaret Thatcher simply followed monarchs and leaders throughout history in whipping up popular support for herself by directing it against an 'enemy' in the form of Argentina. Konrad Lorenz certainly saw the importance of threat from an outside group and argued that one solution was to direct group cohesiveness and aggression into something harmless like rivalry at sport, but this was before the days of football hooligans.

So how can we encourage reconciliation by directing energies in a way that will do no harm? I believe we now need to persuade people that the greatest threat to their own and their children's security is not other groups of people, but rather the environmental threat posed by our unsustainable life style. If people from different groups could unite in fighting for a sustainable way of life for all, we just might be able to encourage reconciliation and conflict resolution, and so move towards a more peaceable world.

~

Empathy

Some years ago a starling hit a glass window at Twycross Zoo and fell to the ground stunned. A bonobo (or pygmy chimpanzee) called Kuni gently picked it up and tried to put it on its feet and encourage it to fly, but it fell over. Then she carefully climbed a tree with her hind legs, cradling the bird in her hands, opened its wings and tried to launch it into the air. But it simply fluttered to the ground. A young bonobo came over to inspect it, but Kuni hurried down and stood guard over the bird for several hours until it had fully recovered and flew off.

Empathy is the ability to understand how another individual thinks and acts; putting ourselves into their place so that we can understand why they think and behave the way they do. It is something that happens all too rarely even among intelligent and well educated people; it is easier by far to expect and demand that others behave in the same way as ourselves. Yet we do not all have the same taste in music nor are we all interested in sport or natural history, so why should everyone behave in the same way?

Unfortunately empathy alone is not enough to make us behave decently. Every so often we read in the press of people carrying out acts of barbaric cruelty, as with soldiers torturing and killing Iraqi civilians. There is a remarkable parallel here with our closest relatives among the apes, the bonobo and the chimpanzee. Male chimpanzees are aggressive with a terrifying dominance display when they charge around tearing up branches and small shrubs, screaming, and woe betide any other chimp, male, female or juvenile, who gets in the way. Low ranking males who do not submit may be viciously beaten up, but dominant chimps can also deliberately seek out and beat up particular individuals they have decided to victimise. And male chimpanzees can stalk and hunt down chimps from a neighbouring group who stray into their territory, beat them up and kill them: chimpanzees often combine empathy with cruelty. Bonobos by contrast usually settle disputes and conflicts by mutual sex, which may be male-female, male-male, female-female or adult-juvenile, and they appear not to take delight in torturing and terrifying others: bonobos combine empathy with sympathy. This is of course a generalisation: not all chimpanzees have this vicious streak in them and not all bonobos show as much consideration for other animals as Kuni, in the same way that we humans are tremendously variable. And while we may feel that the life style of the bonobo is 'better' than that of the chimpanzee, it has not proved to be wildly successful in biological terms: chimpanzees, although under threat from growing human populations, still range from Sierra Leone in the west to Tanzania in the east while the bonobo, as far as we can tell, has only ever lived in a very small area of the Congo forest.

What about the third chimpanzee better known as *Homo sapiens?* We too might be more successful if we combined empathy with cruelty, but the world would be a far happier place if more of us combined it with sympathy. Why is it that so many of our political leaders are so arrogant and self-righteous that they simply cannot understand that other people may have equally valid beliefs and practices to themselves? They seem to be totally incapable of empathy, at least in the international field. Yet if a bonobo like Kuni can demonstrate this quality surely we deserve human leaders who can also show empathy and sympathy?

Flores Man, the 'Hobbit'

The report in *Nature* of 28th October 2004 of the discovery of a new species of human, *Homo floresiensis* or Flores man, popularly known as the 'Hobbit', is perhaps the most remarkable find in the study of human evolution for half a century. Fifty years ago the number of fossil humans and ape-like ancestors that had been found was very small, and they could all be fitted into a simple linear sequence. Some 10-12 million years ago there lived two ape-like creatures *Ramapithecus* and *Dryopithecus*, to be followed by a handful of scantily known fossils until *Australopithecus* 3½ million years ago, *Homo habilis* 2½ million years ago, *Homo erectus* 2 million years ago, *Homo neanderthalensis* (Neanderthal man) 200,000 years ago and ourselves, *Homo sapiens* only 50,000 years ago (although recent DNA studies place the common ancestor of all modern human races at about 200,000 years ago). It was thus possible to see the evolution of ourselves as a steady progression over time as we departed from the body form of the great apes towards that of modern day humans. Our understanding was such that religious people could still argue that somewhere in this lineage there was a sudden disjunction: before it our ancestors were ape-men and pre-human, but after it we were all humans with souls, because this is where God intervened in our evolution. There were conflicting views as to whether there was just one species of *Australopithecus* and one of *Homo erectus* or if there were several. There was also debate as to whether Neanderthal man evolved into ourselves or if we both evolved separately from *Homo erectus*, and whether the transition from *Homo erectus* to

Homo sapiens occurred only in Africa or if there was a steady progression on several continents. But for those with this core belief in the uniqueness of humans and of their place in God's creation there was nothing to disturb their faith. *Homo floresiensis* challenges this sort of belief.

Adult Hobbits at just one metre tall were dwarfs compared with modern people. Central African pygmies are also small (but substantially taller than Hobbits at 1.4-1.5 m), and their skulls and brain capacity are within the normal range for other modern humans. The single known skull of Flores man (actually that of a woman) had a brain of just 380 cm^3 compared with 1,000-1,600 cm^3 for modern humans and 650-1,250 cm^3 for *Homo erectus*. This is even smaller than the brain of *Australopithecus* and about the same size as that of a modern chimpanzee. Yet its skeleton is similar to our own so that it could walk and run just like us. Flores Hobbits lived as recently as from 18 to 13,000 years ago and made stone tools similar to those of contemporary *Homo sapiens* in Indonesia and other parts of the world. This is some 15,000 years after the last Neanderthal man. In Malaysia there are legends and folklore about two 'men of the forest', the orang-utan and the orang-pendek. The first of course still survives (precariously) on Sumatra and Borneo, but has the orang-pendek also survived until recent times? In Flores villagers talk of 'ebu gogo', a short, long-haired primate which may still survive in remoter parts of the island. Sadly if any do still survive they will almost certainly die out as the remaining forests are cut and destroyed.

Why were Flores Hobbits so small? Many mammals restricted to islands have evolved smaller bodies than mainland relatives, either because there is a shortage of resources (notably food), or because there are fewer predators. In Europe there were once dwarf one metre tall elephants on Malta and Sicily. Flores, too, had a dwarf elephant, but it also had a Komodo dragon which would have been a serious danger to the diminutive Flores humans. Similar dwarf humans may well have occurred on neighbouring islands in Indonesia, but few of these have been searched at all thoroughly. Contemporary *Homo sapiens* was already a boat-builder and traveller, but it seems unlikely that Flores Hobbits would have evolved such dwarf stature had they been capable of building boats to regularly travel across the sea to neighbouring islands.

However, startling discoveries in anthropology rarely come without controversy, and the Hobbit is no exception. Just three days after publication in *Nature*, an Australian scientist not associated with the discovery suggested that the small skull was caused by a pathological condition known as microcephaly. He argued that it was remarkably similar to a microcephalic skull from Crete dated 4,000 years ago. Then an Indonesian anthropologist, who had borrowed the skeletal remains and who agreed with the microcephalic explanation, locked away the material so preventing others from examining it. Recently it has been shown that the Hobbit's brain is similar to that of a microcephalic and that nearby villagers on Flores are also small, one man only 1.3 m tall, all of which is consistent with the microcephalic skull explanation. Furthermore the tools associated with the skeletal remains are similar to those of Neolithic *Homo sapiens*. There are now remains of 9 individuals, all small and unfortunately with only one skull, but a second lower jaw has close similarities to the original jaw which differs from that of modern humans in having a bicuspid root to one of the premolar teeth. The debate will no doubt continue until more skeletal remains are found and it is probably still too early to decide if the skull represents a population of small humans or a single microcephalic individual.

Homo floresiensis is certainly unique, and even if it proves to be not as remarkable as its discoverers thought, it is just the most recent of a series of discoveries of fossil humans and ape-like forms over the past 50 years. It is no longer possible to envisage a single lineage of ape-like ancestors gradually evolving into modern humans. The great apes split off from our human lineage 5-6 million years ago. Then from 3½ to 1 million years ago there were a series of ape-like primates in Africa (the australopithecines), some heavily built, others much more slender and agile (the robust and the gracile forms), all living contemporaneously and representing at least two distinct species. Some of the gracile *Australopithecus* probably evolved *via* an intermediate form (sometimes called *Homo habilis*) into *Homo erectus* while the more herbivorous robust ones all eventually died out. Similarly there were a variety of types of *Homo erectus* living from 2 million to 500,000 years ago, but whether these belonged to just one very variable species or to half a dozen distinct species (i.e. which could not interbreed) is uncertain. But for more than two million years in Africa and Asia there were undoubtedly several species of hominid living in the same environment, perhaps in competition with one another, yet sufficiently different such that neither outcompeted the other and caused it to die out. One of these types evolved into modern humans (*Homo sapiens*), another into *Homo neanderthalensis. Homo floresiensis* (if it is not a pathological condition) may have evolved from a third form of *Homo erectus* who somehow reached the island of Flores but was unable to leave it. Our ancestral lineage over the past five or ten million years was probably rather like that of fossil horses or elephants: an ancient form evolved into a series of different types (more than a hundred in the cases of horses and elephants), much as a tree trunk produces several major boughs, and then these in turn evolved into many different species (the branches coming off the main boughs). The twigs all over the surface of the tree represent all of the species alive today. If we now draw a series of semicircles centred on the main trunk representing time we can see that at any one instant there may have been a dozen different hominids alive, but as we move towards the periphery of the tree (the present day) the only ones that survive are the great apes (orang-utan, gorilla, chimpanzee, bonobo) and ourselves.

We differ from chimpanzees, bonobos and gorillas in about 2% of our genes, about the same as the genetic difference between a zebra and a horse. Yet while zebras and horses are considered to belong to the same genus (*Equus*), we recognise at least five genera for the great apes and our human relatives (*Pan, Pongo, Gorilla, Australopithecus* and *Homo*). It is neither the morphological nor the genetic differences that suggest we should belong to a different genus to the gorilla; rather it is the nature of some of these genes and the qualities that they determine: language, consciousness, the ability to make and design tools ranging from carefully chipped stone flakes to the most intricate computer.

How many of these great apes and hominids had a comparable brain capacity and intelligence to ourselves? Most of those that we place in the genus *Homo* could make tools which they used for a variety of purposes; and the neanderthals buried their companions together with tools, and even in one case a flower, suggesting an elaborate ritual possibly even a form of religion. *Homo sapiens* was producing highly skilled cave art at least 30,000 years ago, a time when the neanderthals were dying out but well before the demise of the Flores Hobbits. But how many of these humans could communicate abstract concepts in a form of language? And why did language evolve? Language today is mostly used to make small talk, passing the time of day with friends and relatives. Originally it may have replaced the old primate behaviour of mutual grooming to cement bonds of trust and friendship so essential for successful group-living. Neanderthal man had similar brain size and hyoid apparatus in the throat to ourselves so he too probably had the capacity to develop language. Did the neanderthals (and the Flores Hobbits) communicate using a language? Did they have conscious thought? Could they communicate feelings or recall incidents which happened in the past to their companions? These are the characteristics that distinguish us from the great apes, but we have no means of telling if any other hominid shared them or at what stage in our evolution they appeared. Recent research indicates that the genes affecting our brain evolved very quickly, but it does not tell us if this occurred 50,000 or 500,000 or even 5 million years ago. Nevertheless it is becoming increasingly clear with each new discovery that the characteristics of self-consciousness, intelligence and language that distinguish us from the great apes are ones which we probably share with many of our pre-*sapiens* ancestors and relatives.

~

Fairness

We have heard a lot about fairness recently: is it fair for bankers to be rewarded with millions of pounds every year? And are the Government cuts affecting everyone 'fairly'? What do we really mean by fairness and where do our ideas of fairness come from?

Some readers may be disturbed by the experiments described below because they feel that apes and other primates should not be kept in captivity, but even if we disapprove of them, we can still learn from these experiments.

Several years ago two capuchin monkeys were each given a pebble and trained to return this to the experimenter who exchanged it for a slice of cucumber. The two monkeys soon learned to return the pebble repeatedly until they had had enough. Then the experimenter changed the reward for one monkey who was given a grape (a favourite food) while the other still received cucumber. The one with the grape continued exactly as before, but the monkey receiving the cucumber soon lost interest or became agitated and threw the pebble away. It was not 'fair' that his mate got a better reward. Children behave in the same way: 'Mary's got a bigger piece of cake than me, it's not fair'. In neither case did the monkey who received the grape or Mary who had the larger slice of cake offer to share it with their companion. So 'fairness' can be selfish and may also involve envy. Are we upset at bankers (or pop stars, footballers and directors of Big Corporations) receiving huge salaries because we feel we are just as worthy as them? Or is the problem simply that the differential is too large? The Government claims that its cuts are 'fair' because they affect everyone, but of course they have a far more profound effect on the poor who see the wealthy continuing with their extravagant life-style.

Apes, however, are smarter than monkeys: when a bonobo was given several goodies in sight of her companions, she ate a few and then refused any more, gesturing towards her companions who were looking on but separated from her by a cage. Only when they had been given some reward did she return to finish her own. Why was she smarter? Because she realised that when she returned to her companions they would remember that she had taken all the goodies herself and not given them any, so they would give her a hard time. Bonobos and chimpanzees normally share food within their group, though not necessarily with everyone.

In another experiment pairs of capuchins or of chimpanzees, were given a choice of pressing one of two buttons to get a reward, the first button simply gave them a piece of cucumber, the second button gave both them and their companion pieces of cucumber. Almost every time they pressed the second button. They were, at least to some extent, caring for their partner. Only if the partner was a complete stranger did the balance tip towards pressing the selfish button.

So our own ideas of fairness are not a peculiarly human characteristic: they are something inherited and modified through our evolutionary ancestry. Indeed there is evidence of fairness in other social animals besides primates including elephants and wolves. Our own domestic wolf (the dog) can easily be trained to shake hands (or paws) with people. Dogs will do this either with or without a reward, but if one of a pair of dogs is given a reward while his partner gets nothing, the luckless animal shows disturbed behaviour: it may stop raising its paw, turn away and lower its tail, all signs of stress. Fairness then has a selfish component: others should not be getting special treatment while I am not. But it also has a social component in that it pays to be nice to your companions so as to bond the group together. This leads to generosity towards friends and neighbours, not just to family. In modern society our 'group' has expanded from a dozen or so hunters or foragers to hundreds of people, indeed following Jesus's story of the Good Samaritan it can be extended to include the whole world.

~

Theory of Mind

Some years ago at Twycross Zoo, the bonobo Kuni picked up a stunned starling and cradled it in her hands (see *Empathy*). Then after a while she climbed to the top of her tree, opened its wings with both hands, and launched it into the air. The bird had not recovered and fell to the ground where Kuni guarded it from an inquisitive younger ape. Although her attempt to help the starling had failed it seems that Kuni realised that starlings normally fly and that for this bird to do so it would be easier to start from a high point.

This example gives a remarkable insight into the brain of the bonobo. One characteristic that was long thought to distinguish humans from all other animals is known as 'theory of mind', the ability to realise that the content of someone else's mind is different from ones own. But it may be that chimps and bonobos also have a theory of mind. The bonobo Kuni would never have carried a motionless baby bonobo to the top of a tree and thrown it off: she knew that birds behave differently from bonobos.

On another occasion in Arnhem Zoo the chimpanzee enclosure was hosed down and the collection of large tyres were cleaned and hung on a large log to dry. The female Krom noticed water still standing in the innermost tyre on the log and she wanted it. So she pulled this tyre in all directions, but could not move it because of the other six tyres in front of it and a wall behind. After 10 minutes she gave up and walked away. But her nephew Jakie, who she had cared for when he was younger, had been watching. As soon as she gave up he walked over and removed the tyres one by one, then carefully carried the last one upright so as not to spill the water and gave it to her whereupon she scooped water out of it. Helping is not unusual in chimps, but targeted helping, recognising the goal of another individual, implies that chimpanzees also have a theory of mind.

The bonobo enclosure at San Diego Zoo has a moat round it – bonobos cannot swim so this gives excellent viewing for visitors. On one occasion when it was drained and cleaned the keepers then turned on the hose to fill it. But an old male bonobo, Kakowet, came to the window where he could see the keepers and screamed, waving his arms. They went in and found several young bonobos had climbed down into the moat and couldn't get out. A ladder was put in and all climbed out except the smallest who climbed up Kakowet's arm as he leaned over the edge.

Some years later the moat was permanently drained for safety but the outer wall was too high for the bonobos to climb and escape. A chain was hung into the now dry moat so the bonobos could climb up and down whenever they wished. Several times when the silverback Vernon climbed down a younger male, Kalind, pulled up the chain, then looked down at Vernon with an open mouthed play face, slapping the sides of the moat – as if in laughter at making fun of the boss. Several times a dominant female Loretta then rushed to the scene and pulled up the chain until her mate had climbed out.

These examples show very clearly that our closest relatives, chimpanzees and bonobos, are able to see a situation through the eyes of someone else. We can also see this ability developing in our children in their early years. But it is all too easy to ignore it and assume that what we think someone else should do is the right thing to do. Better by far to listen to and understand their perspective before trying to impose our own opinion on them.

~

The eyes have it

My left eye has sadly been removed, but for more than 77 years it has seen some interesting, fascinating and wonderful things. It has seen the majestic Matterhorn, the 'thunder that smokes' of Victoria Falls, the stupendous Grand Canyon and the superb Yosemite valley as well as thousands of lesser but no less wonderful sites in this country and abroad. It has seen prehistoric remains, ancient buildings, superb views in Australia, Malaysia, Panama and Canada as well as in Europe and nearer home the island of Skye, Malham Cove, Dartmoor and the Lake District. It has seen numerous Quaker Meeting houses in Britain, but also in California and Queensland and one which we knew very well in Ghana with pillars instead of walls supporting the thatched roof. It observed a Quaker Meeting in a wooded Nature Reserve in the Tatra mountains of Poland, and both here and in the Ghana Meeting house the surrounding wildlife was a joy: in Ghana it saw a 2 metre boomslang snake in a Bougainvillea being mobbed by local birds while another time brilliantly coloured bee-eaters hawked for insects just in front of us as we sat in silence.

It has seen grizzly bears, lions, emus and elephants as well as howler monkeys with deafening territorial roars, Madagascar's largest lemur, the indri, with its haunting call and Malaysia's black ape, the siamang with its maniacal cackle. It has seen little auks and great northern divers in Plymouth Sound, a wryneck held in my left hand while I sketched it at Dungeness, and the strange bare-headed rock-fowl in its nesting cave in Ghana. Plenty of fascinating lesser lights too: the tropical spider *Dinopis* which holds a square of sticky web between four of its legs and dabs it on to passing insects, lifting them clear of the ground; red Spanish dancer sea-slugs, camouflaged on the reef but graceful when swimming; hoverflies that are almost perfect mimics of bumblebees; eyed hawkmoths that suddenly expose huge dummy eyes when attacked to frighten predatory birds; and the large yellow and brown flowers of the lady's slipper orchid, once reduced by collectors to a single plant in Britain, but now thriving at several sites on the northern limestones. Indeed seeing even everyday insects in the garden is a real pleasure.

It saw King George and Queen Elizabeth at the Essex Show just after the war, with me perched on the fence of a pig enclosure. Later it looked down on a Warsaw street with a cheering crowd as U.S. vice-president Richard Nixon drove past, and a couple of years later it witnessed a superb speech from Kenneth Kaunda at the Trusteeship Committee of the United Nations petitioning on behalf of Northern Rhodesia. In the office of the secretary to the President in Dar-es-Salaam it saw the door open and the man who peeped round had his portrait just above the door as he spoke briefly to his secretary: it was Julius Nyerere, the finest leader in independent Africa at the time who reduced the salaries of himself and of his chief ministers and spent a week every year in remote villages listening to the problems of his people. But more important than any of these are my family: my wife Janet, children and grandchildren, cousins and grandparents – one grandparent who lost the sight in both of his eyes a few years before he died. And the thousands of ordinary folk it has seen over the years: friends and Friends, people one meets in shops and total strangers, because eye to eye contact together with friendly words helps to build up a positive relationship.

However, I still have my right eye which has seen much the same as the left, yet neither eye has any long term record of what it has seen. The memory of all these wonderful sights is lodged a few centimetres away in my brain, and although time can alter details of my memory, most of these will stay with me until I die. So, thank you, left eye, you have served me very well indeed.

CHAPTER 4

Other Animals

Man and Hyaena

We like to think that we humans differ from all other animals in that we alone have free will, whatever that may mean. We have a conscience, and we alone amongst animals can distinguish right from wrong, appreciate beauty, and can foresee the consequences of our own actions. We can carefully assess the pros and cons before coming to a decision. Sometimes we argue that these qualities are God-given and so do not occur in other animals. We may further argue that these qualities are responsible for the various forms of human behaviour and human society which we can observe today and throughout human history. Yet history is a long catalogue of failures to learn from past errors and to take decisions based on

Spotted hyaena

carefully reasoned arguments. It has every appearance of involving the same decision-making processes which occur in other animals. Maybe I am being unfair to historians and statesmen, but consider the similarities in habits and behaviour between *Homo sapiens*, the wise man, and *Crocuta crocuta*, the spotted hyaena.

In the Ngorongoro Crater of northern Tanzania there is a very dense population of hyaenas: 1.7 to the square kilometre, omitting suckling young. The population is divided up into groups or "clans" of between ten and 100 individuals. The clans are fiercely territorial, regularly patrolling and marking their borders and attacking any hyaena from another clan that enters their domain. Territorial skirmishes between neighbouring clans are frequent, sometimes involving mutual displaying, sometimes actual fighting. If an intruder is caught by members of the clan and it cannot escape, it is attacked, mauled, and sometimes killed. Fighting within a clan is, however, rare: it may occur occasionally, since there is a definite hierarchy in the clan, but it has not often been seen. The society is matriarchal, led by one or two large females, and as high ranking females get the best places at kills, so they get more food than do low-ranking females and males. Furthermore, the young of high-ranking females are weaned after only a year, and thereafter they feed on kills close beside their mother, so they grow quickly into strong high-ranking animals. Conversely, low-ranking females continue to suckle their young for eighteen or more months, and their offspring often get little food from communal kills so that they are slow to grow. This makes sense biologically: if there is plenty of food, all will be well, but if there is a shortage of food, instead of all the clan starving and perhaps dying, the lower-ranking ones will starve and die first while the high-ranking ones remain healthy, and so the clan will survive, albeit with reduced numbers. Finally, although there is a vicious intolerance shown to individuals from neighbouring clans, very occasionally a young male hyaena will enter a new clan as a low-ranking member, and so become a member of two clans at the same time.

If we compare this society with that of primitive or modern humans, the similarities are quite remarkable. We too live in groups which we call tribes or nations, and are fiercely territorial with frequent boundary disputes and occasional full scale wars. We also have a social hierarchy in which the "dominant" or high-ranking classes get the lion's share of food or other resources if these are in short supply, and which perpetuate themselves by ensuring that their children receive good food and education and so have a better chance of achieving high-ranking status than do children of low-ranking parents.

But how has the hyaena society evolved? Are all hyaena populations similar to that in Ngorongoro? The answer appears to be that they are not, and that the fierce territoriality of Ngorongoro hyaenas is simply a consequence of the population having outstripped the available food supply. In the Serengeti plains of Tanzania hyaenas live at the density of 0.12 per square kilometre, only one fourteenth of the density in Ngorongoro. On these plains the hyaenas suffer high cub mortality during the season when the big herds of wildebeest and zebra migrate. Some hyaenas follow the migrating herds, others remain in one area, but there are no large clans. There is usually fairly free mixing of individuals when two groups of hyaenas meet, and little patrolling and marking of territorial boundaries occurs. Because of the high cub mortality the adult population remains low and there is plenty of food for the adults which can travel many miles from their dens to reach a herd of wildebeest. On the other hand in Ngorongoro food is plentiful all the year round, so cub mortality is low and the population reaches a level where all diseased and easily caught prey have already been taken and only healthy ones remain. Although surrounded by food, most of the food is able to escape from the hyaenas unless they are in top physical condition. Mortality of adult hyaenas is high and of course any extension of territory at the expense of neighbouring clans means more food may be available for the clan. It follows that the Ngorongoro hyaenas' territorial marking behaviour, inter-clan warfare, and even the feeding privileges associated with high-ranking females have evolved as a consequence of increasing population.

And what of humans? One must, of course, be very wary of drawing too close comparisons between different species of animals, but it may be worth asking the same questions of humans. Our population has increased enormously over the past century. Has this increased the territorial behaviour and the number of skirmishes between neighbouring groups? Are modern, overcrowded people more distrustful of strangers than we used to be? Has increase in population contributed to and helped to maintain our class system of rank and privilege? Are our actions based on rational thought or are they the result of a blend of instinct and experience, as in hyaena society? Can these problems be resolved while maintaining a high population, or is the only solution to try to reduce population so that it becomes easier to break down barriers of race and class?

~

Something nasty in the Pride?

I have often wondered why so many fairy stories have a wicked stepmother or stepfather who ill-treats the poor children. Possibly the death rate 500 or so years ago was so high that remarriage was common and so the step-parent situation was familiar. But do we really have such nastiness inside us? Perhaps we can learn something from that noblest of all animals, the lion, king of the beasts. The pose and majesty of the male lion command our respect, and, like ourselves, lions are social animals.

Each pride typically has one, two or three adult males and five to nine adult females with young up to three years old. The pride occupies a territory of perhaps fifty square kilometres which the males regularly patrol and from which they drive out other lions by roaring, marking with urine, and fighting. There are also surplus male lions or nomads which scrounge a living between the territories of neighbouring prides. Practically all reproduction occurs within prides.

So much for the social set-up. What can we learn that in human terms is praiseworthy? First, males within the pride do not appear to fight over their mates. When a lioness is in heat a single male usually consorts and mates with her. Second, several females in the pride often

Lions consorting

have cubs of similar age and they feed any of the young indiscriminately. Anyone who has tried to persuade a ewe to suckle another ewe's lamb will appreciate how unusual this behaviour is among mammals. In fact survival of lion cubs when births are synchronised is better than when cubs are born at intervals throughout the year, so this co-operation in rearing is of advantage to the lionesses. It is true that the lionesses usually do all of the hunting and actually provide food for the males of the pride, but apart from this little bit of male chauvinism, the pride appears to be organised on an altruistic basis. But is this really so? And why does the pride have a sexual imbalance?

The females of the pride are all related to each other – mothers, daughters, aunts and cousins – and most three-year old females remain in the pride of their birth until they die. A few may be driven out if the pride is too large: these females may be able to find a nomad male and start a new pride if territory is available.

Males, by contrast, are all driven out of the pride at three years old and become nomadic, roaming in ones, twos or occasionally larger groups. When a group of nomadic males finds a pride with old or weak males they attempt to take it over. Take-over battles can be very damaging – a resident male has nothing to lose by fighting almost to the death since without his females he will have little chance of reproducing again or of catching enough food. But the young challengers can afford to wait if the resident males appear too strong – eventually they will try again and succeed in acquiring a pride.

However, males only hold a pride for an average of two years, so if they are to leave many genes to posterity it is in their interest to reproduce as much as possible in this short period of time. Of course a single male will leave more of his genes to posterity than will two males in a pride, but two males will be able to hold on to the pride for longer than can a single male. So it may pay a male to go into partnership with a brother if in this way he can remain boss of the pride for a longer time. Since lions mate hundreds of times for each litter born, it is not worth while for males to fight and risk damage over females, and in any case if the males are brothers half of their genes will be in common. But males need to have descendents quickly after taking over a pride. This they can do by killing off all young cubs sired by the previous pride males. With their cubs dead the lionesses quickly come into heat again. So it turns out that the synchronous births of lionesses in a pride are the result of infanticide by the new males. This behaviour is not unique to lions – infanticide of a similar nature occurs in some monkeys too.

So here we have a rational, biological basis for the wicked stepmother of nursery tales. In the world of the genes the selfish and cruel can win out in the end. We can learn to understand from the animal world, yes, but finding virtues such as altruism among animals is far harder.

~

A total trust

I expect many readers will have watched David Attenborough's blockbuster *"Life in the Freezer"*, and no doubt marvelled at the tenacity with which Antarctic birds and mammals cope with the extreme severity of the climate. But while all normal animals are in a rush to complete their breeding cycle before the onset of winter so that both adults and young can move north away from the fiercist weather, one bird does the opposite and moves south to start breeding in late autumn. This is the largest of the penguins, the emperor penguin (*Aptenodytes forsteri*), in which the male incubates the single egg on his toes throughout two months of permanent darkness and bitter cold. No wonder that Apsley Cherry-Gerrard described his journey to study the huddle of males just before Scott's ill-fated trip to the Pole as '*The worst Journey in the World*'.

Typical song birds, like our own swallows and blue tits, pair up in Spring, and both male and female share in incubating the eggs and rearing the young. In biological terms it pays both male and female to co-operate, since there is a better chance of successfully rearing young (and so of passing on their genes to the next generation) by co-operation than by desertion and leaving the partner to do all the work. But in most of the song birds that have been investigated it also pays to have 'a bit on the side': between 10 and 20% of the young that are reared are not actually fathered by the male of the pair. For the female, it will pay her to mate with a top quality male because then her young will have the best possible chance of surviving. But only a few males are top quality, so if she is actually mated to an inferior male, she may try to slip away from him to solicit a mating with a better quality male nearby. Similarly a top quality male will take the opportunity when his mate is incubating to search out other females, and thus to increase the proportion of his genes in the next generation. Of course inferior males will also try to maximise their contribution to the next generation in the same way, but other females may reject their advances. So while both male and female in a pair need to co-operate, neither can afford to trust the other fully. Males spend much time watching their mates and driving off rival males so as to minimise the chances of cuckoldry.

Back now to the emperor penguin. In autumn they come ashore onto the sea ice and walk 20 or 50 miles to their traditional breeding sites. Here the pairs mate and the female lays a single large egg direct onto the ice. She immediately slides it onto her broad toes for if it rests on ice for just a couple of minutes the embryo will be killed. Her mate then takes the egg onto his toes where he covers it with fluffed out tummy feathers, and she then leaves him and begins the long walk back to the sea to feed. The males incubate their single eggs on their toes until the females return more than 100 days later.

During this time the weather gets colder with icy winds and blizzards, and the sun disappears for nearly two months. The males huddle together for warmth, those on the windward side continually moving round to the lee of the huddle so that all share in facing the worst of the weather. After 114 days the eggs have hatched, but the males are on the verge of starvation for they have had nothing to eat or drink for four months. Eventually the female returns, takes the chick from her mate, feeds it from her crop full of krill, and the male in his turn walks off to the sea. And so all through the Spring the pair take it in turns to feed and incubate the chick or to go off to collect food. The chicks soon grow big enough to be safely left on their own, and as the sea ice melts the distance to the sea gets less. The grown chicks then walk to the sea, and the breeding programme is complete.

Is trust a quality that birds possess? I do not know, but if it is not trust then it is something very similar that these birds must have to a quite remarkable degree. Maybe it is all instinctive, but it is still quite incredible by human standards to place so much trust in ones partner. 114 days in appalling conditions: does it ever cross the mind of the male that his mate may not return? She may have

been eaten by a leopard seal so that he will be forced to abandon the chick simply so that he can survive to try to breed again. Or she may have mated with some other male so that the egg that he has been incubating for 100 days is not actually his. How many human couples go

71

through such a trial of their love and trust? Yet it happens to every single emperor penguin in the Antarctic. Nobody has yet genetic finger-printed emperor penguins to see if any of the males have been cuckolded, but I would be sad if it is not close to zero.

~

The disinterest of the Naked Mole-rat

What is your favourite wild animal? For some it will be a lion or elephant, for others some exotic bird of paradise, or more likely perhaps a monkey or chimpanzee. But I don't suppose one in a million would choose the naked mole-rat (*Heterocephalus glaber*). The name itself is enough to put one off this creature, yet here is a mammal that leads a fascinating though very hidden life.

When social animals are mentioned some people think at once of honey bees or ants, while others will think of a mammal, lions or wolves perhaps, or maybe baboons or gorillas. Each has its unique feature of social behaviour: wolves and hunting dogs bring back food to feed the young of the dominant female, while lionesses will suckle cubs belonging to other lionesses in their pride, behaviour that never occurs in the social primates (apart from ourselves). Co-operation and mutual assistance is the name of the game. But in many ways the most social of all mammals is the naked mole-rat.

Social insects usually have just a single queen (or a king and queen in the termites), and there are several castes of sterile insects, typically workers and soldiers. The majority of social mammals, by contrast, have several breeding females with just one or two males, and all adults play their part in hunting, looking after young and so on. There are no sterile castes, although the wolves and hunting dogs have just a single breeding pair with the rest of the pack slaving for them – until one of the pair dies when another member of the pack takes their place. The exception is the naked mole-rat which is much more akin in its habits to ants and bees.

It lives in a small area of Kenya and Ethiopia in colonies of between 50 and 100. They live permanently underground, but unlike our European, anything-but-social moles, they are true rodents and feed entirely on roots and tubers. So the colony requires an enormous run of tunnels which have to be constantly extended so as to find new sources of food. The colony can probably pass through several generations without any animal ever emerging into daylight, and their eyes are minute, probably incapable of forming a clear image of their surroundings. Their body lacks hair, hence their common name of naked mole-rat. When not burrowing and searching for tubers, the colony relaxes in an enormous heap in the largest chamber of the burrow. The workers help to care for and clean the numerous babies, and they also keep the tunnels clean and take rubbish (including dead colony members) to a central pit where it is dumped out of the way. In addition to the workers, who may be either male or female, there is a larger caste with dagger-like teeth, the soldiers, whose sole function is to defend the colony from attack by neighbouring colonies or from predators such as snakes.

In many ways this social system is one which we might feel is an ideal which we would do well to emulate: workers and soldiers perform their tasks co-operatively and the colony members seem to live without conflict or fighting. They are even prepared to die in defence of the colony should it be attacked by a mongoose or a snake. But altruism in even the best regulated societies in Nature has its limits. In the central chamber lies the enormous bloated queen, almost continuously pregnant or lactating, surrounded by workers who feed her and tend the young. Only the queen and one or two males breed, which they do non-stop until they die. The workers know at once if the queen has died, and some of the younger workers immediately start to grow rapidly in size and in the development of their ovaries. The first to reach sexual maturity then takes over as the new queen, and if two develop equally they fight to the death, or else one may move to the periphery of the tunnels with a group of workers where they block themselves off and start a new colony.

So for all its co-operation and sharing, each naked mole-rat is very definitely looking after number one: if it is an elderly worker or soldier then the best strategy to ensure that it passes on as many of its own genes as possible is to feed, defend and care for all the young, because they share many of its own genes; and if it is a young worker and the queen dies then its best strategy is to grow as quickly as possible so as to become the new queen. True altruism, where one individual risks or sacrifices itself for others who are not close relatives, only occurs in humans and just possibly in a few other social mammals.

~

Elephant thoughts

If I had the choice of being reincarnated as another animal while retaining my own temperament, I might well choose to be an elephant. Aside from some of the apes and monkeys, and perhaps the whales, elephants have one of the most intricate social lives of any mammal, with complex mutually supportive behaviour and remarkably little damaging fighting. Our current knowledge of African elephants is due in large part to the quarter century of study by Cynthia Moss and her colleagues at Amboseli in Kenya.

Elephant family units are led by an old matriarch and comprise her daughters, granddaughters and nieces together with their offspring. Adolescent males leave the family units and live on their own or in all-male groups for most of the time. They are attracted to oestrous females and try to mate with them, but they are easily chased off by the bigger bulls. It is here that serious fighting may occur – big bulls come into musth (with copious secretions from a gland on the head, high levels of testosterone, and heightened aggressiveness and sexual drive) for just two or three months

African elephant

each year. These are the bulls that females willingly accept, and two bulls in musth may fight each other to the death. Such dangerous fights are minimised, however, because non-musth bulls back down, and prime bulls normally come into musth at different times of the year.

But it is the family units that are of most interest. Elephants can express emotions from contentment and pleasure to apprehension and fear, both through their vocabulary of deep rumbles and by a variety of visual signals involving ears and trunk. Each animal can probably recognise several hundred other elephants whom they will meet frequently or just occasionally. Family members are greeted after a separation; the longer the separation the more effusive the greeting, with a balance between friendship and hostility that reinforces the established relationship between the two animals. If a young elephant is seriously injured or is stuck in mud, some of the big females gather round to help with reassuring rumbles and caresses of the trunk as well as more practical nudges and lifting with feet, tusks and trunk.

It is rare to see such apparent concern and cooperative behaviour in a non-human animal. When an elephant dies, its close relatives may guard it from scavenging lions or hyenas for days before moving on, and they inspect dead elephants and long dried skulls intently with characteristic movements and rumblings. They certainly have long memories, both of people or vehicles that have attacked them, and of other elephants.

When the old matriarch dies, her family unit is often taken over by the oldest daughter, or it may split into two smaller units, which maintain friendly relations with each other. But the advantage of the old matriarch is that she alone may have a memory that can see the group through the occasional severe drought. She may have been led to some distant feeding or watering place by an old matriarch when she was young, a place that is only used perhaps two or three times in a century, and she can lead the group there again in her turn.

What passes through the brain of an elephant that displays such behaviour? They show qualities that we normally think of as being restricted to humans. Yet if they occur in elephants, can we really justify deliberate killing of such remarkable animals, whether for a trophy, or because they are destroying crops, or simply for human food?

It is foolish to suppose that if I were reincarnated as another animal I would retain my human brain and character. But if I were given such a choice, yes, I just might come back as an elephant. But preferably a female elephant, and in one of the few remaining reserves where elephants are likely to remain unmolested for the next half century.

~

The ethics of harming animals

I don't suppose many of us give a thought to the small animals that may be killed when our drinking water is filtered and chlorinated, nor to the fate of all the small insects and worms that we slaughter when we cultivate our garden. Most of us swat house flies, horse flies and mosquitoes if we get the chance, zap wasps when they buzz round the honey pot, and squash, drown or otherwise dispose of slugs and snails when these are demolishing our vegetables. We have no qualms about killing fleas and intestinal parasites of ourselves, indeed we prefer them to be dead. And if we keep free range poultry we may shoot foxes and poison rats. Would we do the same to elephants or monkeys if these were demolishing our meagre crop of maize? Can we justify these actions because of human need?

At the other extreme most readers will probably take the view that our closest relatives, chimpanzees and bonobos, should not be killed for food or for medical or any other scientific research. Many will feel they should not be kept in zoos either, and certainly not be permitted to suffer physically or mentally for research even if it is we humans that will benefit from the work. What about monkeys? And the lower primates – lemurs and bush babies? Many people have strong views about using dogs and cats for research which may involve some pain, but what about other mammals including rats and mice? Is their brain and perception of pain any less well developed than that of our beloved Rover? What about birds? Or fish and amphibians? Should we draw the line at vertebrates so that we can do things to invertebrates that we would not permit to be done to vertebrates? If this is the line, what about octopus and squids whose brain and behaviour is certainly as complicated as that of a fish or a frog?

There is no space here to review all the ethical issues relating to killing animals or subjecting them to pain, but it is important that those of us who are concerned with these matters think them out very carefully indeed. I have not even touched on the use of sheep or goats genetically engineered to produce, say, human insulin: animals which are well cared for but whose sole purpose in life is to benefit humans (just as the purpose of domestic cows is to produce milk and meat). Somewhere along the line from *Amoeba* to ourselves there are various lines that we have to draw: animals on one side can be treated in various ways, animals on the other should not. The problem is that it is impossible to know if any animal actually perceives pain. Yes, of course it can respond to it, but does it feel the pain like we do? And of course the Animal Kingdom cannot be arranged in linear fashion from *Amoeba* to ourselves – it is more in the nature of a complex tree with hundreds of thousands of branches of which just a few twigs can perceive pain in the way that we think an ape or an elephant can. We have also to beware that our ethics is not that of the 17th century puritans who objected to bear baiting, not because it gave pain to the bear, but because it gave pleasure to the spectators. Is it ethically right to object to some treatment to a cat, but not object to the same treatment on a rat, because cats are our pets and rats are perceived to be vermin?

I have to confess I simply do not know where I stand on some of these issues. I am convinced that some mammals can perceive pain and that we should do all that we can to minimise human induced suffering to these animals; and I also believe it is prudent to assume that other animals with similar neural and behavioural systems may perceive pain and so should be treated in the same way. Above all I believe that all animals (vertebrate and invertebrate) should be treated with respect, which at the very least means thinking about these questions and ensuring that our actions are consistent with our thoughts.

~

Octopus

Some years ago while searching for sea-slugs in the rock pools off Monterey in California, a friend passed me a baby octopus he had just found. With its eight tentacles extended it fitted comfortably into the palm of my hand. It glided gracefully over my palm and then hunched over my forefinger. Even with my lack of familiarity with octopus behaviour I immediately thought "this is it: it's going to bite me". And it did, just a small nip with its parrot-like beak, but it felt like a bee's sting. After examining it for a few minutes, I released the little animal, but the finger swelled up overnight and was quite bloated for a few days – and even a year later there was still a small pimple to mark the spot.

The octopus appears to some as a scary monster, to others as an animal that is fascinating because it is so unlike any of the creatures with which we are more familiar – such as mammals, birds or even insects. Sir Arthur Grimble, in the colonial service in the Gilbert and Ellis Islands between the wars, described (in *A Pattern of*

Islands) how he joined in a traditional octopus hunt as the 'bait'. It was as well that he was a good swimmer, for he had to swim to a rock crevice where a giant octopus was known to live, and then, holding his breath, he allowed the octopus to emerge and grasp him. The octopus worked its way over his body until it was about to bite his chest. This was the moment his 'partner' in the hunt was waiting for: as the octopus opened its beak to bite, its brain was exposed, and the swimmer bit with his teeth into the creature's head and destroyed the brain.

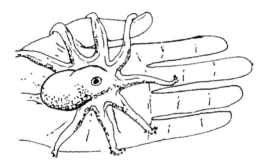

Octopuses are more than just weird creatures with a poisonous bite; their eyes are better designed than our own. In our eye the nerves from the retinal cells pass across the face of the retina before turning down through the retina to the brain, this opening in the retina forming our 'blind spot'. This means that light coming to our retina must pass through the near transparent nerves. In the octopus the optic nerve emerges from the back of the retina so there is no blind spot and light does not have to pass through nerves before it reaches the retina.

Octopuses also have the most sophisticated nervous system and behaviour of any invertebrate animal, on a par with that of fishes and reptiles. In simple feeding trials they quickly learn to associate certain symbols with food, just as can reptiles, birds and mammals. Yet for all their elaborate behaviour they are killed for food in many parts of the world, and few people worry about the way in which they are killed. Slowly humans, at least in Britain, are coming to realise that we should do our utmost not to cause pain and suffering to the most intelligent mammals such as chimpanzees and elephants, and there are over a million members of the RSPB devoted to trying to preserve British birds. But the poor intelligent octopus, and its relatives the cuttlefish and squids, have no protection, and are killed in enormous numbers every year throughout the world. Most people give little thought to accidentally or deliberately killing pest insects or slugs: they have such small brains that it is exceedingly unlikely that they 'suffer' in the way that an injured mammal probably suffers. But what about the lowly octopus and its relatives? Do they perceive pain in the same way that we do? We simply do not know, but in the absence of knowledge maybe we should treat them with the same respect we show to mammals and birds?

~

Meerkats

I am sure that many readers of *The Friend* will have seen the outstanding film *Meerkats United* on their TV screens several years ago, and more recently the soap series *Meerkat Manor*. The life of one remarkable female meerkat, Flower, has recently been documented in a book by the lead researcher on the meerkats of the Kalahari, Tim

Clutton-Brock. The remarkable characteristic of meerkats is that in a very short time the animals habituated to the presence of the human researchers who could sit beside them and follow them on their daily foraging trips. Many were even weighed each day without being alarmed in any way, and sentinels often used the head of a watching researcher as a sentry post to scan the horizon.

Meerkats are ultra-slender cat-sized social mongooses with dark shadowed eyes and a delightful alert posture when scanning for predators. The success of the group requires that every individual cooperates with each other but at the same time the males need to explore and perhaps infiltrate neighbouring groups as they will not mate with their close relatives. Each day different individuals stay home to look after the young until they are old enough to follow the group as it forages for food, and a female nursemaid will suckle the cubs even though she is not their mother. While foraging some of the older meerkats take spells on sentry duty to warn the group of eagles or other predators, and both nursemaids and sentinels pay the price of their altruism by being unable to feed while on duty. When the pups are older and follow the group they beg for food, and the older meerkats to whom they beg will give them a prize grub or scorpion that they have just spent several minutes digging out of the sand. But first thing in the morning when they are hungry the adults always eat any food they find and only then do they give food to begging pups – they look after number one. And if a rival group trespasses on their land the meerkats give a threatening war dance and may have to fight to defend their territory, injuring or even killing the intruders.

Occasionally a female who is not the dominant leader of the group will become pregnant (from a roving male belonging to another group), and pregnant females are very aggressive. If two females are pregnant, the pups of the first one to give birth are usually killed by the second female within hours, but when her own young are born the whole group, including the female whose young were killed, accepts them and will nurse them.

So meerkat society has many traits that, in humans, we would consider admirable, but other traits that we would find unacceptable. The soap-opera *Meerkat Manor* differs from *Eastenders* and other soaps in that the actions were not scripted: the cameramen simply filmed what happened and the script was then written by the producer or a script-writer. But Tim Clutton-Brock as lead scientist was careful to edit the script: words like 'aggressive', 'worried' or 'friendly' are perfectly acceptable because one can judge this from the animal's behaviour, but he crossed out words like 'love', 'hate', 'generosity' and 'trust' because these are emotive human terms and we simply have no idea whether they have the same meaning for a meerkat. Indeed it is very difficult to be sure whether a dog or an elephant or a chimpanzee – or any animal apart from ourselves – is capable of these emotions. Yet it is precisely these emotions that are so important in our own lives and in human society because they can over-ride the dictates of natural selection and selfish genes. In the natural world killing your nieces or your neighbours will become wired into your genes if it increases the chances that your own genes will persist in future generations, but hopefully we are more than mere biological machines.

~

The Elephant Whisperer

Grief is the sadness that we feel when someone close to us dies. It is very difficult to know if other animals experience grief in the same way that we do because they cannot tell us what they feel, so all we can do is observe their behaviour and try to interpret what we see as objectively as we can. If one of a pair of dogs who have been together for many years dies, the survivor's behaviour will change implying that the partner is really 'missed', and a cow whose calf has been removed can bellow continuously for several days. This may be interpreted as grief but there is no evidence that it persists for very long as it can with us. If a new male lion takes over a pride he will try to kill all of the cubs sired by the previous male; the lionesses may try to hide their cubs or even to threaten the male, but after the cubs have been killed there is no behaviour among the lionesses which can be interpreted as grief, and they very soon mate with the killer male. Elephants, however, are different.

When an elephant dies the family group may return to the site a year or more later when all that is left is the larger bones, and they then spend some time delicately feeling the bones with their trunks. This is quite different from their behaviour with the long dead skull of some other animal: they seem to know that the elephant bones belonged to a member of their family whom they knew well in life. When someone close to us dies we feel great sadness, but we can also appreciate modern funerals which celebrate happy memories of our deceased friend because these memories can never be taken away from us. It seems that the elephants may also have been remembering their dead friend.

Horse whisperers are exceptional people who are able to talk quietly and confidently to injured, terrified or traumatised horses to calm them down. Lawrence Anthony lived on the enormous Thula Thula Game Reserve in South Africa and was known as the Elephant Whisperer because he had this ability to relate to elephants in the same way that horse whisperers do to horses. Some years ago a Game reserve some 600 miles away asked if he could take a small herd of elephants which had developed the habit of breaking out of their enclosure through an 8,000 volt wire fence and causing havoc on local farms, otherwise they would all have to be destroyed. They arrived at Thula Thula, terrified from the long journey, and the matriarch charged up to the fence in a most aggressive manner if anyone approached it, threatening to break it. The Elephant Whisperer spoke quietly to her through the fence, telling her not to do it (as the whole herd might then have to be shot), that he would befriend them and that this was now their home. After an hour or so she backed away, taking the others with her. Lawrence then spent much of his time close to the herd, talking to them, until eventually the matriarch approached him calmly and extended her trunk through the electric wire to feel him. After that he regularly approached them in the Reserve and was greeted in the same way with no hint of aggression.

Some time later Lawrence Anthony died. By then there were two herds of elephants in the Reserve both of which were friendly with him. A few days after his death one herd arrived just outside his house after a journey of about 12 hours. The other herd arrived the next day, and all of the elephants stayed quietly for a couple of days before making their way back into the bush. The behaviour of the elephants when they realised that their friend Lawrence Anthony was no longer around implies that they remembered him. Of course we have no idea if elephants can feel anything akin to sadness and sorrow, but their behaviour does suggest that they recalled important memories of their friend.

If elephants and possibly other highly intelligent mammals such as chimpanzees, bonobos and dolphins are capable of grieving then we should treat them just as we treat fellow humans who are grieving, with love, patience and understanding. Grief may not be a uniquely human emotion but be something we have inherited from our pre-human ancestors.

~

Rogue Elephants

Some while back a televison documentary told the tragic story of the savaging and killing of cattle in Uganda and of rhinoceroses in South Africa in 2006-7. A large number of animals were killed but this did not appear to have been caused by poachers – rhinos are usually killed by poachers for their valuable horns, but all of these animals had their horns intact. In South Africa the incidents were in the Pilanesberg National Park to the west of Johannesburg, where over a couple of years more than 50 animals were killed. The surprising thing was that only rhinoceroses were killed and none of the freshly killed animals was eaten by whoever killed them. In Uganda the situation was similar except that the animals killed were domestic cattle close to the Queen Elizabeth National Park. In both cases the cause of death was deep stab wounds on the back of the animal. After a considerable amount of time and patient research it was discovered that the culprits were young male elephants.

Male elephants live in bachelor groups and from time to time one or more of them develop a hormonal condition known as musth, characterised by copious secretion of fluid from glands on the temples and excessively aggressive behaviour. Musth elephants fight far more aggressively than normal elephants and two animals in this condition may fight to the death. They fight in order to gain mating rights with any females in the area. The bull elephants in Pilanesberg were all comparatively young and came into musth much earlier than is normal in other places such as the Kruger National Park. The reason for this was that Pilanesberg was only established in the early 1980s at which time there had been no elephants in the area for perhaps a hundred years. It was decided to capture elephants from Kruger where they had enormously increased in numbers and translocate these to Pilanesberg to start a herd there. But at that time it was only possible to tranquillise and move young animals by lorry. Typically cow elephants were shot and killed (because there were too many of them) and the young calf was then caught, manhandled onto a lorry, and released with others in Pilanesberg. Here the herd of young animals grew to maturity, but every one had been traumatised by witnessing the death of its mother and its own capture. The situation in Uganda was similar except that here the elephants were slaughtered by Idi Amin's soldiers for meat and ivory, only the young being left to escape because they lacked ivory tusks. So both areas had populations of traumatised elephants lacking an experienced matriarch to lead them when they were young, and the adolescent males lacked the presence of older bulls to follow as they grew older. These young males then went into musth much too early: normally the presence of older, larger bulls seems to inhibit the onset of musth for perhaps 10 years. The young males then tried to court any largish animals in the area that did not run away, rhinos in South Africa and cattle in Uganda. But these animals did not respond like real elephants and somehow released an aggressive streak in the elephants which stabbed down on them with their tusks, crushing and killing them.

In our own species there have recently been men in the United States and elsewhere who have become violent attacking and killing scores of innocent people who happen to be nearby. Is there anything we can learn from the behaviour of the rogue elephants that might help us to understand and possibly prevent such terrible occurrences in humans? In the cases of the rogue elephants in both South Africa and Uganda it was the destruction of the stable, social community which caused the problem: the young elephants lacked the behavioural interactions and experience of their mother and aunts and so grew up maladapted to elephant life although it would have been impossible to predict that they would resort to killing other animals. Not personally being a specialist psychologist it is impossible to generalise, but it does seem that these men had all suffered some dreadful unhappiness leading to deep-seated resentment, for example break-up of the family home, bullying or resentment at a teacher who was perceived to pick on them. This unhappiness coupled with the ready availability of guns or knives and the boost to the ego of feeling in control of the terrible situation seems to have overridden the normal friendliness and tolerance we feel towards other people.

CHAPTER 5

Evolution and Genetics

Darwin and Natural Selection

2009 was the 200th anniversary of Charles Darwin's birth and the 150th anniversary of the publication of his best known book *The Origin of Species*. But what sort of man was he and what precisely is meant by 'Natural Selection'?

Darwin was born into a comfortably wealthy family so he had an assured income throughout life. At Cambridge his academic career was not particularly outstanding, but in 1831 he was offered the opportunity to join *H.M.S. Beagle* as a companion for Captain Fitzroy on a voyage round the world carrying out survey work. In South America he found fossils of marine fish high up in the Andes, and on different islands of the Galapagos he noticed the physical differences between populations of mocking birds and giant tortoises.

On his return Darwin settled into a life of academic study and married his first cousin Emma Wedgewood. It was a happy marriage and Darwin was evidently a father who took time to enjoy playing with his numerous children. While Emma was a practising Christian, Charles was probably more of a journeyman, but it was the slow and tragic death of their daughter Annie that finally caused Charles to lose his Christian faith. At that time the standard Christian belief was that God created everything and could intervene in the world, but Darwin could not reconcile the concept of a loving God with a God who could let Annie die so tragically.

Darwin was a sensitive and humane man: as a medical student he was horrified seeing patients screaming as operations were performed without anaesthetics, and in South America he witnessed the appalling treatment of slaves. He was convinced that all humans of whatever race were essentially the same, contrary to the popular view that different races had been created differently.

Meanwhile Darwin's academic studies continued with monographs on barnacles and other animals contributing to his reputation as a serious scientist. Over nearly twenty years he developed the idea which formed the basis of *The Origin of Species*. By 1850 many scientists accepted that species had changed (or evolved) over time, but the process by which this happened was a mystery. Darwin's contribution was to explain how animal and plant species could evolve; his theory had four simple postulates:

All organisms are variable – no two rabbits or cabbages are the same;

All organisms produce more young than can possibly survive to adulthood (a fact that he picked up from an essay by Thomas Malthus);

Because of this high mortality only the best adapted individuals will survive to reproduce – this is what is meant by Natural Selection;

The characteristics of the surviving individuals are inherited by their offspring.

If this looks like commonsense, then so it is, indeed Thomas Henry Huxley thought it was so obvious that he really should have thought of it himself. But its consequences are far-reaching: it implies that all animals and plants have evolved by gradual change and adaptation to their environments in successive generations from much simpler organisms: it explains how evolution has occurred. Just one thing remained unexplained and that was the mechanism by which characteristics of individual animals and plants were inherited. This had to wait until 1900 when the work of Gregor Mendel more than 30 years earlier was rediscovered: these characteristics are controlled and determined by genes which are located on chromosomes in the cells of the body, and of course we now know that genes are composed of units of DNA. So biologists now know that animals and plants have evolved over the past four thousand million years from the first living organisms, that they have evolved through the processes of environmental change and natural selection, and that evolution and extinction are now more rapid than for at least 65 million years because we are so drastically changing our environment.

~

Natural Selection or Intelligent Design

Many of the evangelical Christians on whom President Bush relied for his re-election believe that all animals and plants were individually created. Some even believe that they were all created in 4004 B.C. and no amount of reasoned argument or presentation of scientific information on fossils and dating of rocks will change their minds. However, in recent years a new movement has emerged in the United States which is a more serious challenge to Darwin's theory of organic evolution: the view that animals and plants have evolved by 'intelligent design'.

Advocates of intelligent design believe that organisms are so complex that they must have been designed by some higher intelligence. This theory is similar to that of Paley, 200 years ago, who considered that the eye is so complex a structure that it is inconceivable that it could have evolved gradually. How can part of an eye have any useful function without the rest of it? Therefore the eye must have been designed, and if it evolved gradually this is because the designer chose to do it this way.

Fossils show that extinct animals once roamed the earth and thus there has been a process of organic evolution, but advocates of intelligent design believe that this process has been directed by the designer. The designer is God, though not necessarily the Christian God, for it could equally be the Islamic God or the Jewish God – or indeed a Quaker God, for I guess that many Quakers believe in some form of evolution by intelligent design.

There are two scientific arguments that can be used to refute the theory of evolution by intelligent design. First, exploration of the theory of natural selection to explain structures such as an eye. If one starts with animals insensitive to light, then the initial stage in the evolution of an eye might simply have been a mutant with a light sensitive chemical enabling it to move towards or away from light. Over many generations this simple behaviour became more complex and the light sensitive chemical became concentrated in a specific structure or eye.

The next stage may have been formation of a vague image so that the animal could detect a shadow (a possible predator). Only later did a lens and retina evolve so that the form of the image became more precise. Every stage in this gradual evolution of a complex eye would have given its possessor an advantage over its fellows with simpler eyes – there is no need to postulate either instantaneous creation of a complex eye or gradual evolution not supported by natural selection. Incidentally our own eyes (and the eyes of other vertebrates) are badly designed optically because the nerves emerge from the front of the retina. This means that light must pass through the nerves before it reaches the retinal cells; the eye of an octopus is potentially better than our own because its nerves emerge from the back of the retina. Would an intelligent designer God have designed an eye with such an elementary flaw?

The second argument against intelligent design is demonstration of evolutionary changes actually occurring by means of natural selection over a few years or a few decades: the classic example is industrial melanism in peppered moths (*Biston betularia*). The black (melanic) moths increased from rare mutants 150 years ago to dominate populations in industrial areas of Britain by 1950. Typical moths are better camouflaged on soot-free tree trunks covered with lichens while melanics are better camouflaged on blackened trunks. Bernard Kettlewell and others showed that insectivorous birds prey on the more conspicuous moths, so these birds are the agents of natural selection which has brought about this evolutionary change. Then, following the Clean Air Act in the 1960s, typical moths have spread back into areas from which they had been displaced. Similar changes have occurred in more than 100 different species of moths in industrial Europe, North America and Japan.

Thousands of similar evolutionary changes have occurred in the past 50 years in organisms ranging from mammals and insects to flowering plants and bacteria, for example repeated spraying of crops with insecticide has resulted in hundreds of species of insect pest evolving resistance to these chemicals. It is difficult to believe that all of these changes were directed by God: if they were, then God decided on evolution of all of these pests which attack our crops, transmit diseases and parasitize domestic animals and ourselves. It is hard to reconcile such a God with the Christian God of love.

If the path of evolution has indeed been directed by God (as Paley and the intelligent designers believe) then there should be examples of evolutionary change *not* brought about by natural selection. But every example of evolution studied can be explained very easily by means of natural selection.

Sometimes people say that evolution is purely a matter of chance, but this is not correct; the initial mutations which occur in every individual that has ever lived are random, and it may be a matter of chance whether it is you or I who gets run down by a bus or eaten by a lion. But in population terms it is those individuals who have certain beneficial genes who have the best chances of surviving to reproduce and pass their genes on to the next generation. So the available evidence points to natural selection being overwhelmingly the most potent force in driving the direction of evolution.

So is there a conflict between science and religion? The Darwinian theory of evolution does not deny the existence of a God, although many of its present day publicists like Richard Dawkins are atheists. The answer to this question depends on ones definition of God. If God is a supernatural force, the creator of all life, who planned the evolution of humans, then, yes, there is a conflict because there is no evidence from biology indicating that some force other than natural selection has been involved.

If God created a system that works without interference, simply allowing the natural laws of the universe to operate rather than intervening from time to time to ensure that evolution follows a predetermined direction, then there is no conflict; but this God must also be responsible for evil and for the tuberculosis bacillus and the malarial parasite. However, if God is the spirit of love and truth in our hearts and is irrelevant to the creation of the universe and the evolution of living organisms, then there is no conflict with science.

~

Working with Genes: perils and possibilities

When I walk into town to shop I sometimes see a man, whom I will call John, close to the Emmaus community hostel for the homeless where he sleeps. He must be in his late 30s, and he lurches in an alarming and uncoordinated way on the pavement. Pedestrians who do not recognise the symptoms tend to cross the street, like the levite, to pass by on the other side. But John is not drunk; he suffers from Huntington's chorea. This debilitating condition typically affects people in their mid-thirties and within three or four years they die. The condition is caused by a single dominant gene (Hc). By the time that the symptoms develop the sufferer is very likely a parent, and half of his or her children (on average) will inherit the condition. One of the hopes for families that have Huntington's chorea is that genetic engineering technology may be able to help. First, unborn foetuses in families where the condition is present could be screened for presence of the Hc gene. If the foetus is affected, then the parents have the ethical decision to make of whether to give birth to a child who will die by the age of forty, or whether to terminate the pregnancy and so eliminate the Hc gene from their family. Second, but in the more distant future, it may be possible to replace the Hc gene in the young child with a normal gene so that s/he never develops the condition.

Multinational chemical companies are now inserting genes for herbicide resistance from bacteria into crop plants such as oilseed rape and cotton. The plants can then be grown free from competing weeds by spraying with that particular herbicide: it will kill all the weeds but not the resistant crop. Farmers may welcome the development because, although the seed will cost more, it should be easier to keep down weeds. But it is even better news for the multinational and for its shareholders since they will hold patents on both the herbicide and on the transgenic herbicide-resistant seed. They will obviously try to promote it as the best thing since DDT so as to maximise sales and profits. But will it really benefit farmers? The

Irish potato famine was particularly disastrous because farmers grew a single clone of potatoes; had they grown a dozen different varieties the chances are that a few would have had some resistance to potato blight and so enabled them to produce at least some food for their starving families. Genetic diversity of crop plants is important as a safeguard against disease and adverse weather conditions.

It is common knowledge that many multinational pesticide manufacturers continue to promote their products when it has been clearly shown that they have damaging environmental effects or even when they fail to control the targeted pest. So how can this misuse of genetic engineering technology be prevented?

The ethical issues involved in these two examples of genetic engineering are, I suggest, clear, and I have no doubt at all how I would respond if I were asked about the benefits of these proposals. For other examples the issues are far more complex. The important thing is that all genetic engineering projects should be debated in ethical terms before they are allowed to proceed. There is some hope that this may happen in the nations of Western Europe and North America, provided that Quakers and others continue to pressurise their Governments. But a host of commercial applications of genetic engineering technology are taking place now in several small Asian countries with no safeguards at all as to what is and what is not ethically acceptable.

How can we assess if a genetic engineering proposal is good or bad? I suggest what is needed is a simple cost-benefit analysis, but one in which the currency is emphatically not money. First, evaluate the benefits of the proposal in terms of gains in scientific knowledge, human well-being or long term environmental benefit. Then assess the costs in terms of, for example, possible harm to people or suffering to another animal, or of danger to the environment. Finally we need to weigh the costs and the benefits. If there is little overall benefit, or if the costs are unduly high, then the precautionary principle should apply, and the proposal should not proceed.

The stakes are high: the benefits of genetic engineering could be enormous, but so could the disasters.

The last time I saw John he was being helped to stand up by a friend. It looks as though the terrible disease is now running its inevitable course.

~

Genetic Engineering in Plants

Most people see no ethical problems with plant breeding, that is, the careful crossing of different varieties so as to give plants with (for example) disease resistance or increased yield. Similar crop improvements can be brought about by genetic engineering, e.g. by isolating a gene from one variety of a plant, such as wheat, and then inserting it into the genetic make-up of another variety of wheat. While genetic engineering was used to make this change, it could have been done through standard plant breeding methods, although it would have taken several years longer. A more complex example of genetic engineering is the recently introduced tomato which remains firm for weeks: the gene which causes ripening has been literally 'turned round' (inverted) so that the enzymes that cause over-ripening are not formed, and the tomato now stays firm for much longer. Such gene inversions also arise naturally by the occasional inaccurate copying of the genes (this is one form of mutation), but the chances against this one specific inversion arising naturally and being picked out by a horticulturalist must be many billions to one, so this tomato could not in reality have been produced by conventional plant breeding.

Genetic engineering can also be used to move genes from one plant to another plant belonging to a different species (for example from wheat to potatoes). This sort of change is again one which could never be brought about by conventional plant breeding methods. An example of where such a change might be useful is where a community is dependent on one food plant which lacks important amino-acids (e.g. potatoes in andean communities). It should be possible to design a gene for a specific amino-acid which is absent in such a plant, and to insert this gene into cultivars of the plant. The 'improved' crop would have a beneficial effect on the health of the people. However, if the 'improved' seed had to be bought anew each year it could make the community heavily dependent on the whims (and profit motive) of a commercial company. Similarly, improvements in yield of plant products such as pyrethrum could be brought about through genetic engineering.

It is also possible to isolate a gene from a microbe or an animal and then introduce it into a species of plant. For example, 'transgenic' tomato, tobacco and oilseed-rape plants have now been engineered which have resistance to a herbicide, the resistance genes coming originally from micro-organisms. This means that the crop will survive spraying with this particular herbicide but the surrounding weeds will be killed. Chemical companies are developing this method because they can patent the transgenic seed as well as the herbicide, and thereby make a handsome profit. Tobacco, cotton and other plants have also been engineered which contain genes from a bacterium (*Bacillus thuringiensis*) that produces toxins which kill certain insects. If these insects now eat the transgenic plant they will die. Another goal of genetic engineers is to introduce genes for nitrogen fixation from micro-organisms into commercial plants as this would reduce reliance on fertilisers. This appears more acceptable ethically than herbicide resistant plants, but it may not be of great value: plants that expend energy on fixing nitrogen are likely to put fewer resources into flowers and fruit, so will give poor yields.

Genes from one microbe can easily move into other microbes through natural processes, but such 'lateral' transfer of genes between species of higher plant and animal is much rarer. However, it does occur, e.g. through *Agrobacterium* which causes crown galls on many species of plants. A genetically engineered form of *Agrobacterium* could be used to transfer the engineered genes to all the different species of plants that it infects.

All genes that are moved from one organism to another take with them a 'marker' gene which enables the scientist to recognise easily which of the plants have been successfully engineered and which have not. Although there is no intention that this gene should have any harmful effect on the plant concerned, or on people who eat it, there is a possibility that it may occasionally do so.

Another area of concern is whether genetically engineered plants will escape into the environment and 'take over'. Recent experiments with transgenic oilseed-rape suggests that it loses out in competition with normal rape, and also that high yielding strains of rape lose out in competition with naturally occurring wild plants. However, pollen from a transgenic plant can fertilise closely related varieties or species in neighbouring fields so that the engineered gene can spread. Whether it will persist in such populations for more than a few years remains unknown.

In summary, there are benefits from genetic engineering of plants, but it is important the principal beneficiaries are the local farmers rather than the chemical manufacturer, and that any possible harmful side effects are evaluated and eliminated.

~

Genetically modified foods

What are GMOs?

Careful selective breeding of domestic animals and plants over the past few thousand years has resulted in many different breeds of cattle, poultry and dogs as well as high yielding varieties of cereal crops. But there are limits to what traditional breeding can achieve: it can only select for genes present somewhere in the population of the species involved, and (with rare exceptions) it can never introduce genes from a different species. Bacteria and viruses can do better than this: they can transfer genes very easily from one species to another, indeed it probably happens every day. Molecular biologists can now make similar transfers, not only between micro-organisms, but between higher plants and animals as well. They can now cut out a specific gene from one plant (or a bacterium, or an animal) and insert it into another one, thereby making a genetically modified organism (GMO).

The potential of this gene technology is enormous: to restrict consideration to food plants, it is now (or soon will be) possible to insert genes for frost resistance or salt tolerance into crops such as tomatoes so that these can be grown in arctic or saline soils. Food plants can be engineered to include genes that make insecticides so that when they are attacked by greenflies or caterpillars, these will be killed. With ever more human mouths to feed world-wide, genetically modified (GM) plants could give the necessary boost to food production that is needed to prevent mass starvation.

Where are they being grown?

In 1998 74% of all commercially grown GM crops were in the United States, and if we add in Canada, Argentina and Mexico this rises to 99%. In Britain 300 ha of GM crops (mainly oilseed rape) was grown as part of experimental trials. This year too (1999) the only GMOs grown in Britain are for experimental purposes.

Are GM foods safe?

One problem with any gene transfer is that a gene with a specific function in one organism may act differently in another. And while most GMOs are probably harmless when eaten by us, there are some with genes for an insect toxin (designed, for example, to kill caterpillars) which might have a more harmful effect on ourselves. Every GMO contains, in addition to the target genes that have been transferred, one or more marker genes (to enable the scientist to check that the transfer has taken place), and often promoter genes as well. The markers are frequently antibiotic resistance genes. Bacteria in the environment or in the intestines of ourselves or of domestic animals will, occasionally, pick up this gene so that they become resistant to the antibiotic. We are already suffering from too many human pathogens that have evolved resistance to antibiotics, and the use of such marker genes may enable still more bacteria to develop antibiotic resistance.

Should GM foods be labelled?

It is very difficult to know if food you buy contains GMOs because the United States refuses to distinguish between GM and normal crops, and most processed foods do not tell you the source of all of their ingredients. However, EC Regulation 1139/98 requires that all new packaging of products which contain GMOs (including GM food additives) must be clearly labelled 'genetically modified'. The British Government is planning to enforce this regulation shortly. There are also plans to insist on similar labelling of GMOs used in animal foods, but this may take some time.

Are there environmental dangers?

Many of us may have worries about the safety of GM foods, and about whether they should be labelled, but the issue of most relevance for wildlife conservation is whether GMOs will have harmful effects on the environment. Several currently used GM crops contain genes for resistance to herbicides, e.g. oilseed rape in this country and soya in the United States with genes for resistance to glyphosate. The farmer can spray his rape field with glyphosate to kill competing weeds without harming the crop. However, pollen from oilseed rape (*Brassica napus*) occasionally fertilises wild turnip (*Brassica rapa*, a common native weed), so there is a chance that herbicide resistance can be transferred to populations of wild plants. The published evidence as to whether this will occur is conflicting, but if increasing acreages are planted then over a decade herbicide resistance will certainly enter the gene pool of local weeds so that these can no longer be controlled by herbicide.

GM crops with genes that make insecticides are now being developed: one contains genes that make scorpion venom so that the plant will kill insects that eat it. The advantage of these to the farmer will be that he has no need to spray with an insecticide, and it has been claimed that this would result in reduction in use of insecticides. But the disadvantage of all GM crops is that they are likely to lead to reliance on a small number of genetically similar crops in monoculture. It only needs a new pest to appear for the entire crop to be at risk – this is what happened 150 years ago with the potato famine in Ireland. We already have enormous fields of single crops with virtually no weeds and few species of insect, and this has led to a decline in such once familiar birds as tree sparrow, skylark and partridge. Increased use of GM crops will exacerbate this situation leading to a further reduction in biodiversity and putting the small populations of these birds at still greater risk.

Who benefits from GM crops?

There is little doubt that large agribusiness farmers will gain from growing GM crops: they can afford the seed and herbicide, and weed-free crops give higher yield than weedy crops. But the biggest gain will be for the manufacturer who will have patented the GM crop. If the manufacturer does not also make the herbicide he will link up with the multinational who does, and they can then corner the market for that particular crop. The competition is cut-throat: multinationals are now experimentally inserting 'terminator' genes into plants so that farmers cannot save seed from GM crops because they will be sterile. This ensures that fresh seed has to be bought each year from the multinational.

There is still a dream in the eyes of supporters of GMOs that the technology can substantially increase the food produced in the developing world and so help to ward off starvation. But peasant farmers could never afford the seed. Multinationals even now are using FAO money to give seed and chemicals (pesticides and fertilisers) to African farmers free. The catch is that the farmer has to buy fresh seed (and chemicals) the following year. This practice is disastrous: once peasant farmers have lost their local 'land-races' of crops, developed and selected over hundreds of years, all it needs is one bad harvest with the new crops and they will be destitute.

CHAPTER 6

Places of interest

The Worship lingers

I stood and looked at the Buddhist temple of Sam Poh in Brinchang. The Malaysian tourist information handout about the area asked people to respect the temple, so evidently some do not. My own reaction as I looked at the bronze statues, in front of which were little piles of oranges, glasses of some drink, candles and smouldering sticks of incense, was similar to that in York Minster: appreciation of the craftsmanship and a feeling of respect because of the faith that others give it. Yet early Friends would have been horrified at such sensitivity to a steeplehouse, and no doubt at the temples of other religions. While I do not believe a temple or church is holy in itself, I do think that some of the faith that others express imbues it with holiness. It is similar to the feelings that were expressed by T. S. Eliot about houses in *The Family Reunion*:

'In an old house there is always listening, and more is heard than is spoken.

And what is spoken remains in the room, waiting for the future to hear it.

And whatever happens began in the past, and presses hard on the future.'

So the faith of those who have worshipped in religious places passes on to those of us who come after.

I would have thought that, as a Friend, I should have preferred the plain white mosques to the ornate Buddhist and Hindu temples, but I did not. Was it the craftsmanship and carving that I was admiring in the latter? Was I being inconsistent with my beliefs? Friends reject symbols because they get in the way of what those symbols are trying to express, and so come to be worshipped for themselves, rather than for what they represent. Do Friends lose something by this rejection? Might we be expressing an unwarranted superiority – that we can manage without the help that others need? My own feelings are mixed. Take the way we talk about light, for instance. We use the powerful metaphorical image of the 'inner light'. There are Friends who say they have had a wonderful spiritual experience in candlelit meetings. We often light candles for vigils. And yet the use of candles as symbols is not found in normal meetings for worship. But they are powerful symbols not only for other Christians, but for many other religions too.

While in Malaysia, in addition to wondering if Friends are being arrogant or missing something by not using symbols, I felt that much of Christianity, especially the Protestant forms, are lacking in the everyday importance of religion. In Malaysia there are small shrines and spirit houses everywhere. Little red boxes with open fronts stand by the road, always with a few oranges and sticks of incense.

Those who are Buddhist or Hindu have small shrines in their houses. Religion pervades life, temples are social and cultural meeting places. This can be true to some extent in Catholic countries, especially in southern Europe and Latin America, where a crucifix on the wall of the house may have candles in front of it, and religious festivals are important social events. In these groups, religion brings joy into people's lives. But in the more fundamentalist groups such as some forms of Protestant Christianity and Islam, while it may sometimes be a communal activity, important in everyday life, it is austere and not celebrated with joy.

And for many Christians in the Anglo-Saxon world, including many Friends, religion is just one facet of an increasingly compartmentalised life. Our work, our house, our health, our education, the system of ruling the country, and also our religion are all separate, unlike the simpler society in which humans evolved, where they grade into one another. Even though Friends say our faith is for seven days a week, not just one, how much is this really so?

Some years ago a teenage group in a Friends Meeting made a questionnaire that they put to adult Friends. One question was: "Do you always have grace before meals, or only when Sewell comes to tea?" for Sewell Harris, a greatly respected and much loved Friend, religion permeated his life far more than it does for most of us. How many of us only practise our religion in the prescribed Meeting for Worship or if we think that other Friends may see us?

Janet Edmunds

~

An Impression of Kenya

A land of stupendous contrasts: hot, humid coast and baking semi-desert to intensively farmed western highlands; urban tower blocks and squalor in the slums to the savannas and forests rich in plant and animal life; wealth and affluence to the peasant farmer and the desperately poor in the shanty-towns; the greed of the rich and the envy and violence of the desperate to the generosity and kindness of people in all walks of life.

We all carry away with us unique experiences of this wonderful country and its diverse people; what follows can only be personal. My friends in Nairobi warned me of the danger of mugging and robbery in the city and by the roadside (they had been robbed six times in four years). The guidebook warns of tricksters in Nakuru who discreetly pour oil in your car axle and then offer to mend the leak at their garage. My friends kindly lent me a Daihatsu four-wheel-drive vehicle, and two men in Nakuru who waved me down were more concerned at a front wheel wobble than an oil leak. Though costly, this seemed no swindle at all – but on returning to Nairobi, I discovered my mistake. And near Kitale, returning from birdwatching on a toll road I found that I had lost my 10 shillings for the return toll. What could I do? Eventually the toll collector's assistant came with me the few miles to where I was staying to make sure I returned with the money. He turned out to be a Quaker from Chavakali. Another contrast: the reluctance of the collector to trust anyone and the welcome and trust of one Friend to another.

The roads vary from smooth tarmac to the most atrocious, which require four-wheel-drive, but most good ones have frequent colossal potholes and the most lethal head-cracking 'sleeping policemen' in villages, often without any warning. These bring speeders down abruptly from 60 to less than 6 mph. The natural vegetation and animal life is fast being reduced to a handful of forest reserves and national parks. There are plantations of exotic trees in the cool highlands: these resemble Scotland with heavy mist and stretches of pine and fir, but the odd cackle of the crowned hornbill betrays their tropical location. Kenya has 'islands' of wildlife, each containing plants, insects, birds and even monkeys that occur nowhere else in the world. Then there are the sheer mass of birds on the soda (alkaline) lakes and of grazing mammals with their predators on the plains. But even in Nairobi one of the most haunting memories is the cacophonous call of the Hadada ibis. The lesser life is also fascinating, from yellow-striped brown chameleons to the enormous number of different insects. But how much will survive the next century? Will the contrasting styles of human life be equalised upwards? And if so what will be the cost?

On our first evening, before most Friends arrived on the Nairobi bus, our worship was drowned by a tremendous tropical storm, reminding us that we are just a small part of the natural world, and that if we wish our children to thrive we must work with the natural world, not against it. To destroy for quick gain will do irreparable long-term damage. The greed of the rich and the poverty of the poor combined together can easily lead to disaster. The triple problems of population, resources and development need urgent attention if this jewel of a land is to be saved for the next generation.

~

Dreaming over Africa

A day-time flight of ten hours over the length of Africa gives plenty of time for musing over what is happening below. The Sahara, two hours of apparently lifeless red sand, devoid of people, some smooth with occasional ripples, some with star-like pimples, in reality enormous dunes. Not all is lifeless, as there are scattered settlements and tracks. Nobody can sustain a living here so these must be military or mining enterprises.

And now two hours of Sahel, more varied with root-like branches of dried-up rivers and rocky cliffs and gorges; with sparse settlements and a scattering of minute black dots, each one a tree. These coalesce into woodland near the Niger river. Will it ever be possible to transform this parched landscape into a granary as the northern edge of the Sahara once was for Rome? Unlikely: the water table is too low, irrigation leads to salination, and the sparse vegetation is overgrazed by countless domestic animals. How can the world feed the millions of new mouths that are born every year in Africa, a continent that suffers from a succession of famines?

I last crossed the western Sahara 24 years ago when we lived in Ghana, at that time a country that was steadily improving the lot of the citizens so that starvation and malnourishment were rare. A few years later the situation deteriorated and malnourishment became widespread. But today we are flying further east, over Nigeria, the most populous country in Africa, whose current rulers' oppressive policies are a far cry from the mutual help that followed the tragic civil war in Eastern Nigeria a generation ago.

On over the dry hinterland of Cameroon, and the cloud now obscures the moister forested country as we pass into the night. Over to the left is the Central African Republic, a sparsely peopled land whose murderous ruler, President Bokassa, has recently died. Below us now are the hidden forests of Cameroon, Gabon, Congo and Zaire: for how long will these wonderful forests survive the onslaughts of mega-timber companies, hell-bent on extracting every tree as quickly as possible because dollars matter more than the health and wealth of the land and its people?

Zaire – a giant in a state of tragic disintegration, with its sick despotic ruler spending much time in Europe, unable to help and lead the people. Over to the left lie the graves of millions of murdered people in Rwanda and Burundi, the surviving refugees are either returning to their home villages, still in fear for their lives, or trekking deeper into Zaire, in the hope that they can scrape a living there. Would that the return of refugees were the final act of this long drawn out tragedy but, alas, it will only be the final act for those who die; the bitterness and suffering are likely to persist for many years yet.

Angola, another huge country rent by years of civil war and at last striving to pull itself out of the mire. The outcome is far from certain. Now we are skirting Zambia, across the Caprivi strip – relict of some ancient colonial politicking – and the sparsely populated Botswana. Everywhere, if I were on the ground, I would see resilient African women with food or with firewood on the head and picken on the back. If only the African male politicians had some of the qualities of these women the continent might be in a much happier state.

What a depressing commentary on human progress and development. True, there are pockets of hope, usually involving self-help schemes, though one has to read the less well known literature to learn about them. Africa is full of courageous and resilient people. But it seems to take two steps forwards and three back. Is there any hope for this seemingly doomed continent?

Now we are coming in to Johannesburg. I was last here 29 years ago after more than two years working in Ghana, flagship of the alternative to apartheid. South Africa then seemed to be the worst country of all, with its commitment to apartheid. But now it is a beacon of hope. True, the rand is not worth what it was on the foreign exchanges, and crime and drugs are rampant, but many Afrikaners and virtually all black people see things as improving.

How can a country once so committed to injustice and racial domination shake off the hatred that these policies fostered? Much is surely due to the character of one man, Nelson Mandela. A ten-hour flight is tedious, but it is nothing to a quarter-century in prison. How many men could emerge from so long in prison with so few signs of bitterness and hatred?

There are still tremendous problems and people are impatient to see solutions soon. But here at its extreme tip and in the most unlikely country of all, there is cause for hope in Africa.

~

Pendle

Perhaps the commonest image of Pendle is shown from the north, seen from near Sawley or travelling along the A59 from Clitheroe to Skipton. For our Golden wedding in New Year 2013, our family gave us a lovely painting of Pendle, painted by our daughter's partner. It was viewed from the south, which would have been the way George Fox approached it when he climbed up from Barley. At first I had difficulty in recognising Pendle in the painting. This made me think of how our perceptions change when we view the same subject from a different position. The significance of Pendle will vary for different people. For Quakers it is important because of George Fox, who climbed it 'with much ado' and had a vision of a great people to be gathered. Most Lancastrians will associate Pendle with the Pendle witches, a group of local people in the early seventeenth century, who suffered from the persecution meted out to those who were accused of witch-craft, and for some of them because they were Catholic. The incident was popularised in a novel in 1951 and is now used as a tourist attraction. For those who like

116

Pendle Hill

hill walking, it is a distinctive hill of millstone grit and shale, separated from the main mass of the Bowland Fells. For bird watchers it is where dotterel stop on their way to summer breeding in Scotland. We all have our own view of Pendle, none is the only correct one.

The same is true of many aspects of life. Different people can look at the same situation from a different perspective and each may be equally valid. We need to be careful when judging those who see things differently to us. We lived in Ghana for ten years. There, and probably in some other parts of Africa, one does not send an acceptance to an invitation to a party, only regrets if one cannot go; it is assumed that people will go to a party. If one receives two invitations for the same time one accepts the one which one considers the more important, rather than the one which was received first. This can easily lead to misunderstandings. If an English person apologises for not accepting a Ghanaian's invitation because of a prior engagement, to the Ghanaian this would mean that the prior engagement was thought to be more important. On the other hand a sound, very like what we call a wolf whistle, is just a normal way of trying to communicate with someone from a distance, and has no unpleasant connotation. An English person should take no offense from it. We all need to be aware that different people may have different views and perspectives on life.

Janet Edmunds

~

Return to Hill House Meeting

On 6th October 2002 I attended Hill House Quaker Meeting, exactly 39 years to the day since my wife Janet and I first attended in 1963. We then attended regularly with Janet serving a term as clerk until we returned to England together with our daughters in August 1973. So what has changed in the past 29 years? The roof of the Meeting House is no longer thatched but tiled, and the old wooden pews have been replaced with exceedingly uncomfortable wood and concrete ones which so far have been too heavy to 'walk'. Trees have grown up so that when 'I lift up mine eyes' I can no longer see the hills, and the shrub by the Meeting House, where once a host of small birds scolded a boomslang while we sat in silent worship, has gone. The more or less equal balance between Ghanaian and expatriate Friends has changed: today there are a larger number of regular attenders, almost all Ghanaian and almost all male. The entrance has an imposing gate, and nearby where there was once a portable table and chairs for children's meeting while their parents worshipped, there are now no children: unless wives can be attracted to Meeting as well as husbands, children are unlikely to come.

Ghanaians are just as friendly as they have always been, from taxi drivers and security men to people encountered in offices and on the street. It was a pleasure to be greeted so warmly by former students at Legon who remembered both Janet and me, and who are now professors and senior lecturers. At the university student numbers have rocketed to twenty-four thousand, and there has been a similar massive increase in provision of higher education throughout the country. People are growing more food in their back yards, a small contribution towards making the country self-sufficient and reducing the cost of imports. Where there are no buildings, almost the entire land between Accra and Koforidua is now cultivated with cassava, maize and paw-paw together with pineapple, cocoyam and cocoa in the moister places. Only a handful of giant forest trees and the odd pocket of lower shrubs remain in this farmed landscape, but it will be interesting to see if the loss of forest cover has any longer term adverse effects on local rainfall and soil quality. A small oasis of forest remains round the dramatic Boti Falls on the Pawnpawn river so this delightful spot still attracts tourists, but two other almost as fine waterfalls between Boti and Koforidua are entirely surrounded by farmland so are much less attractive to visitors.

By far the biggest change in the 29 years, however, is the increase of Ghana's population from 7 or 8 million to 18 million today, in 2002 (26 million by 2015). Accra has engulfed everything out to Achimota, Legon and beyond: the plain leading to the hills which once had just the odd small village is now submerged in Greater Accra. In another 29 years how many Ghanaians will there be? More than 40 million if the rate of increase remains the same. Can the land provide sustenance for this enormous number of people? Has anyone thought about it and should Friends be concerned? Efforts over the past 50 years to alleviate poverty and suffering have cut the percentage of the population who are poor, but the actual number of poor has increased because of the larger population. Many years ago an old Christian evangelist Prempeh Nunoo occasionally came to Meeting. When I learned that he had a large family I gently suggested that this might be too many his reply was 'God will provide' What wonderful faith! I had no answer then, but today I would remind him that 'God has no hands but ours', and if we want 40 or 50 million Ghanaians we must work out how we are going to feed and clothe them all, keep them healthy, and provide the TVs, mobiles and internet facilities they will want.

Hill House Meeting

The great challenge for all of us in the next few decades, wherever we live, is how to bring our population into balance with the capacity of the earth to sustain it. Our aim must be to improve the lot of all those living now without compromising the potential of the land and its resources to sustain our children and grandchildren. We are called to love our neighbours, neighbours being everyone we meet as well as those we try to avoid meeting. By 'loving', I mean caring for them, ensuring that they have enough food and other essentials so that they too can learn to love and care for their neighbours. What sort of environment should we aim for that will best enable us to care for each other in this way over the next 29 years?

CHAPTER 7

Population and Ethics

People versus the World

1991 has shown us all too tragically that warfare still plays a part in the politics of the modern world. The east-west conflict has lessened, but north-south conflict remains, and there are a host of local wars. No doubt they will drift on for many years yet, but the really big conflict that we are facing is that between people and the world. This is the environmental crisis and its effects are deforestation, desertification, pollution and global warming. It is more difficult to understand than are traditional wars because the two sides are less clearly defined: it is pressures from the increasing mass of people and their increasing demands that are placing the stability of the world's natural systems in jeopardy. To that extent there are two sides to the conflict, but it is a war with no winners. If the mass of people continue to destroy the world then we will all lose out, and the only way the world can win (and retain most of its complex physical, chemical and biological systems intact) is for the people to withdraw some of the pressures they currently impose. Here I want to explore some of the insights from my professional study of ecology and from our Quaker faith.

A basic principle of ecology is that the majority of animal populations increase rapidly to a limit imposed by their food supply and then crash. So in many populations a number of individuals are actually on the edge of starvation. This limit is called the 'carrying capacity' of the environment. But many animals manage to regulate their numbers slightly below the carrying capacity by means such as territory. Most garden birds stake out breeding territories which ensure that they have an area free from competitors in which to collect food for their young. Those that hold territories have just about enough food, while those that lack territories must move away and very likely not attempt to breed at all. Other animals, like lions and chimpanzees, hold group territories and exclude other individuals and groups from their regularly patrolled range. Such groups usually have enough food for their needs within their territory.

The second principle from ecology is that long established ecosystems have higher carrying capacities than environments created or altered in recent years by people. A savanna National Park in Africa can sustain a higher weight of grazing native animals than can adjoining land used for cattle (even when this land is 'improved' with fertilisers). This is because of its greater diversity of animals with different feeding specializations: zebras eat the coarser grasses, gazelles the finer ones, some antelope graze while others browse and giraffe crop from tall trees. By contrast cattle can only eat some of the vegetation, and if we add sheep and goats these actually tear out some plants by the roots and so destroy the vegetation. In Amazonian tropical forest it has recently been calculated that fruits, nuts, fibre and other natural products harvested sustainably from the forest can provide a greater financial income than felling timber on a cyclical basis or conversion to cattle ranching. Furthermore, this income goes to local people in local markets, not to rich businessmen in foreign exchange. In both of these examples the attempt to alter the ecosystem for the benefit of people actually degrades it so that it can produce less. Pollution similarly reduces the potential of ecosystems to produce organic matter.

However, although undisturbed ecosystems are normally more productive than ecosystems altered by people, we cannot always utilise the richness of a natural ecosystem. Much of Britain, for example, was originally oak-ash forest, providing plenty of timber but not much food (acorns are not very palatable), and it may actually be more productive in human terms to convert it into a field of wheat. What we have to try to do is to modify ecosystems so as to maximise their carrying capacity of products that we can utilise: food is clearly of prime importance, but wood, cotton and medicines are other valuable products that we need. This can best be done by altering the natural ecosystem as little as possible. Drastic changes are likely to alter the climate (especially in the tropics) or the soil; they will almost certainly reduce the diversity of animals and plants that can live there, and also reduce the carrying capacity of the land.

Why, then, do people destroy their environment when it is in their long term interest to protect it? In part it is lack of knowledge and understanding, but two other reasons are greed and poverty. The greed of the rich leads them to take now and to hell with the future. The poverty of the poor means that basic survival takes priority over all else – a scrap of food or firewood now is a matter of life or death even if it degrades the land for next year. And the affluence and advertisements of the rich stimulate the desires and envy of the poor. We should remember that the rich are not just Paul Gettys and yuppies because on a world scale virtually all of us British Quakers are very rich indeed. Gandhi said: "There is enough for everyone's need, but not enough for everyone's greed". But very soon there certainly will not be enough for everyone's need: indeed there may not be enough now, in 1992.

Now for the insights from our faith. We cannot today believe that animals and plants were created by God primarily for our benefit. No, they have evolved through the same natural processes by which we have evolved. Have we the right to destroy them? I am not discussing here whether it is right or wrong to kill a cow or to swat a fly, but is it right deliberately to destroy an entire species like the African elephant, black rhinoceros, giant redwood, corncrake or even a host of different sorts of butterfly? One can argue that we should not destroy species of plant or animal because we may find some use for them, a valued drug perhaps, or because they give us pleasure, but really the question is an ethical one. I would suggest that we have no more right to wipe out the elephant or the dodo than we have to destroy a city or a people. The trouble with this principle is that for the poor of the third world the national parks are often seen as land that could provide food from crops or game. Is it right to preserve a few remaining rhinos at the cost of people starving? It sometimes seems that there is a straight choice between destruction of habitat with extinction of animals and plants so that the land can be used for food, or of preserving the habitat while allowing people to starve. However, if local people are involved in a national park, and gain financial benefits from it, they are enthusiastic and effective wardens.

On ecological and moral grounds, therefore, it would be far better to limit our numbers below that at which we are forced to destroy the wonderful array of animals and plants around us. But how can we halt population growth? We cannot surely approve of the draconian legislation in parts of China which prohibits more than one child per woman. Is there another way that will work in the few years we have in which to solve this problem? In many cultures provision for old age means ensuring that one or more children are there to look after the parents. Because some children die of illness or starvation it is necessary to have several children. If the standard of living is raised by genuine community development and health care, people will feel more sure that their children will survive, and they also will come to see the advantage of spending their limited money on educating and caring for just a few children. We in the affluent west need to press for debt cancellation to allow this to occur. We need to give funds to allow the currently unmet demands for family planning to be realised. Empowering women and educating communities will allow people both to understand the pressures on the environment, and to take appropriate action at the family level. Every child should be a wanted child with a good chance of surviving the early years of life.

But we need to do more than just focus on the family. Our own future and well-being are intimately tied up with the future of the rest of our planet. We can only achieve a decent life for all people on earth if we learn the lessons so well-known to many (though not all) societies in the Americas, Africa and Asia: they exploited their environment on a sustainable basis so that both it and they could thrive year after year: they had a deep religious faith based on the natural world. We have lost these beliefs and practices. Yet it is only by working with the natural environment, not against it, that we can have any hope of sustaining the six billion people currently alive on earth, let alone their children and grandchildren.

~

People versus Creation

"We are deeply rooted in the complex matrix of interrelated living forms and processes of the earth, yet we are acting as though we were separate from this matrix and are steadily destroying its fabric. Would creation be better off without us?" (Anne Brewer)

Would the world be a better place if humans vanished from the face of the Earth? Certainly the consequences would be profound: for more than 99% of all animal and plant species their populations would increase because they currently suffer from human activities, while just a handful ranging from potatoes and brown rats to hookworms and human fleas would become rarer or even go extinct. But would the world be a 'better place'? Surely this is a value judgement which implies a better place for we humans irrespective of other animals and plants? And surely too a better place for humans is a worthy objective, so long it is for *all* humans and so long as it is *sustainable*?

There is no doubt that humans so dominate life on Earth and have so profoundly altered every single ecosystem that the populations and well-being of almost all other species have been harmed. But does this matter?

Simple ecosystems like those in the arctic are liable to violent fluctuations from year to year: snowshoe hare numbers increase geometrically to a peak every 10 or so years and then crash with knock-on consequences for the arctic foxes and snowy owls that are dependent on them for food. Lemming numbers in the boreal and vole numbers in Britain have similar but less dramatic fluctuations ever three or four years, but these have less severe consequences for their predators because these usually have alternative prey. In the tropics the occasional epidemic that may devastate one species will have much less of an impact on other animals. This is because there is a much greater diversity of animals and plants such that a change in one species has much less effect on others here than it does in the arctic. Simple experiments in artificial ecosystems in the laboratory confirm that the more species that are present the less likely it is that one or more will go extinct. This is why biodiversity is so important: high biodiversity promotes stability of populations and enables a greater biomass of different species to thrive. So if we promote vast areas of monoculture (of just one species such a wheat or spruce) then it is likely to be under much greater threat from pests than is a mixed planting of half a dozen crops interspersed with species-rich grassland and scrub. It is claimed that monocultures provide more food per hectare for our expanding human population than do mixed species cropping, but this may not be true if the long term consequences to the soil of repeated monoculture cropping are taken into account.

A further reason why biodiversity is important, and why conservation groups are right to strive to save tigers, rhinos and other threatened species, is that unusual animals, plants and ecosystems delight and uplift the human spirit. Life would be so much duller without primroses, song thrushes and all the other animals and plants that have declined as a consequence of modern farming practices.

Natural ecosystems are self-regenerating; if a tree falls down because of a hurricane or because it is felled by a beaver, then the gap is quickly filled by a host of younger trees most of which eventually die as the canopy is gradually restored. Farmed ecosystems may also regenerate into forest if they are left fallow for many years, but today much agricultural land is so altered by chemicals and heavy machinery that the natural succession has been profoundly altered. In some places we have so polluted the land that it will take hundreds of years for it to return to something like its original state. Indeed we have now so polluted the atmosphere that the climate is itself changing so that the original ecosystems may have gone forever. Of course ecosystems have been evolving for millions of years, so this is nothing new, but what is new is the *speed* at which environmental change is happening. There simply is not time for most animals and plants to adapt and evolve into new forms better able to cope with changing conditions.

Humans have a habit of seeking short-term gain even if the long term consequences are disastrous – this is what most politicians offer us and it is also what most people seem to want even if they are unhappy with the main political parties. Two well-known examples are the Roman Empire and the Easter Islanders. North Africa was once the granary of Rome, but today it is largely desert and semi-desert. Although natural climatic fluctuations may have played a part in this change, it is almost certain that bad farming practice and cutting trees, which led to increased evaporation and decreased rainfall, also contributed to the disaster. In Easter Island the people cut down all of the trees for boats and other purposes, and then they were trapped with no possibility of evacuating and finding another more hospitable island. Today in many countries the soil is being degraded by over-cropping and farming methods that are not sustainable, even though they may provide more food in the short term. We face an almost impossible dilemma: attempting to feed and give good quality of life to as many people alive today as we possibly can – but at the same time reducing the potential of the land to sustain such populations in the future; or improving our treatment of the Earth now for the long term good of humankind – but accepting that there may be reduced resources available for people alive now. The trouble is we simply do not know what is the sustainable carrying capacity of the Earth for humans. We know that wild populations sometimes increase beyond the capacity of the environment to support them, and they then crash. We want to avoid this catastrophe for ourselves because of the personal suffering it would cause, but we really must plan for future generations as well.

If humans are to survive another few thousand years then everything we manufacture will need to be recycled, from concrete and glass to plastics and chemicals. In the long term quarrying of stone and minerals and landfill for refuse disposal will need to stop. And we will need to limit our expanding population to the level that can be sustained by the Earth's resources indefinitely. Nobody knows if that means a world population of four, ten or fifteen billion (we are currently at just over six billion), but the means by which we limit our numbers needs to be thoroughly debated. Most animal populations expand until cut back by starvation or disease; we surely would prefer to stop increasing before we reach that stage. But how can it be done? The tawny owl points to one way. In vole plague years owls lay 3 or 4 eggs and most of the young will fledge successfully, but in the year of the vole crash they lay just one egg or even refrain from breeding at all. How can this system work successfully? Surely the occasional selfish owl that laid eggs in a crash year and was successful (because so few owls would be competing

 to feed families) would pass on genes for such behaviour to their young, so that this habit would increase in the population as a whole? The answer is that female owls only lay eggs if the male has stockpiled food for her incubation period. If he cannot supply enough food she lays only one egg or none, and the pair will simply feed themselves for that year and try to breed again the following spring.

If tawny owls can limit their families to the available resources, surely we with our greater intelligence and remarkable technology should be able to do the same? But the natural world is selfish, and it is normal for the strongest and the better competitors to out-reproduce the weaker. Our own history is much the same with the rich and powerful families and nations seeking to maximise their use of resources at the expense of the poor. Do people have to behave in this selfish way? Or should we also be seeking for a more equal sharing of the world's resources?

Notes and references

Chapter 1: Flowers

The Beauty of Flowers: *The Friend* 1991 March 22: 371-2.

To give pleasure: *The Friend* 1994 March 18: 328.

Monkshood: *The Friend* 2014 March 7: 3.

Love-in-the-mist: *The Friend* 2014 October 31: 3.

Double Flowers: 2015.

Chapter 2: Insects

Ants: *The Friend* 2000 March 17: 6.

Contemporary Slave-raiders: *The Friend* 2000 March 24: 6.

Pax Argentinica: *The Friend* 2002 January 18: 6. The exploits of the Argentine ant are summarised by David Queller in *Nature* **405**: 519-520 (2002).

Wasps: *The Friend* 2003 October 3: 9.

How doth the little busy bee?: 2005.

Chapter 3: Primates

Delinquent Chimps: *The Friend* 1985 September 6: 1145. See also article by Jane Goodall in *National Geographic Magazine* **155**: 592-621 (1979); and *The Chimpanzees of Gombe* by Jane Goodall, Belknap, Harvard (1986).

Our aggression and its Animal Origins: *The Friend* 1988 December 23 & 30: 1649-1651.

Behaving like a Baboon: *The Friend* 1990 January 19: 83-84. See also *Almost Human* by Shirley Strum, University of Chicago Press, Chicago (1987).

Human origins: *The Friend* 1991 March 22: 382-383.

On Being Human: *The Friend* 1991 April 5: 434.

Thirty Years with Chimpanzees: *The Friend* 1992 January 31: 143-144.

Monkey business: *The Friend* 1998 September 25: 7-8.

Empathy: 2006. Much more information on bonobos, chimpanzees and human nature can be found in *Our Inner Ape* by Frans de Waal, Riverhead Press, New York (2005).

Flores Man, the 'Hobbit': 2006. See Rex Dalton in *Nature* **431**: 1029 (2004), Daniel E. Lieberman in *Nature* **459**: 41-42 (2009) and Kate Wong in *Scientific American* **16**: 48-57 (2006).

Fairness: *The Friend* 2011 December 16: 3. For more on fairness among animals see *The Age of Empathy: Nature's Lessons for a kinder Society* by Frans de Waal, Souvenir Press, London (2010).

Theory of Mind: 2015. For more about Theory of Mind see *Primates and Philosophers, how morality evolved* by Frans de Waal, Princeton University Press, Princeton & Oxford (2006).

The eyes have it: 2016. *The Quiet Word* (Leeds AM Newsletter), January: 6. Also in Lancashire C & N Newsletter 2016.

Chapter 4: Other Animals

Man and Hyaena: *The Friend* 1975 August 1: 885-886.

Something nasty in the pride: *The Friend* 1979 September 14: 1147-1148.

A Total Trust: *The Friend* 1996 March 29: 15.

Naked mole-rat: *The Friend* 1996 May 3: 7.

Elephant thoughts: *The Friend* 1997 April 4: 11-12.

The Ethics of harming Animals: 1998.

Octopus: *The Friend* 2000 April 7: 6.

Meerkats: 2009. See *Meerkat Manor: The Story of Flower of the Kalahari*, by T. Clutton-Brock, Weidenfeld & Nicholson (2007).

The Elephant Whisperer: 2015.

Rogue Elephants: 2015.

Chapter 5: Evolution and Genetics

Darwin and Natural Selection: *The Friend* 2009 February 13: 12.

Natural Selection or Intelligent Design: *The Friend* 2006 January 20: 10-11.

Working with Genes; Perils and possibilities: *The Friend* 1995 July 7: 855-856.

Genetic engineering in plants: 1997.

Genetically modified foods: *Lapwing*, Magazine of the Lancashire Wildlife Trust, summer 1999: 12-13.

Chapter 6: Places of interest

The Worship lingers: *The Friend* 1989 April 21: 485-486.

An Impression of Kenya: *The Friend* 1991 September 6: 1143.

Dreaming over Africa: *The Friend* 1997 January 31: 7-8.

Pendle: 2014

Return to Hill House Meeting: 2002.

Chapter 7: Population and Ethics

People versus the World: *The Friend* 1992 February 7: 172-174.

People versus Creation: *The Friend* 2001 June 29: 7-8. See also Anne Brewer, *Earth Quaker* 35, p. 6,